THE BIBLE AND ANCIENT TRUTHS

Andrew Killick

Reader, All Saints Church, Preston on Tees,
and Retired Head of Classics at Yarm School, North Yorkshire

First published 2022

Destinworld Publishing Ltd
www.destinworld.com

© Andrew Killick 2022

All rights reserved. No part of this book may be reprinted or reproduced or utilised in any form or by any electronic, mechanical or other means, now known or hereafter invented, including photocopying and recording, or in any information storage or retrieval system, without the permission in writing from the Publishers.

British Library Cataloguing in Publication Data. A catalogue record for this book is available from the British Library.

ISBN 978 1 8380086 1 1

Cover design by John Wright

In this book, except where otherwise stated, all the Biblical quotations are taken from THE HOLY BIBLE, NEW INTERNATIONAL VERSION®, NIV® Copyright © 1973, 1978, 1984, 2011 by Biblica, Inc.® Used by permission. All rights reserved worldwide.

Biblical quotations marked RSV are taken from the Revised Standard Version of the Bible, copyright © 1946, 1952, and 1971 the Division of Christian Education of the National Council of the Churches of Christ in the United States of America. Used by permission. All rights reserved.

Translations from Classical authors are by Andrew Killick, except for the William Johnson Cory translation of a poem by Callimachus in chapter 20.

Dedication

This book is dedicated to my grandchildren Sam, Holly, Caleb and James, with the hope and prayer that they may enjoy these stories and grasp these ancient truths.

Many thanks to all those who read early drafts or contributed in other ways to this book, including...

Jeremy Atkinson, Jayne Davies, Gillian Davison, David G C Emerton, Lucy and Matthew Falcus, Angela and Peter Gray, Sue Jennings, Chris Kettle, Ruth Kettle-Frisby, Karen Killick, Robin Killick, Scott Linnett, Walter Moberly, Lance Pierson, Alan and Anne Rolfe, Hazel and John B L Taylor, Janet and John Taylor, Pauline Taylor, Alister Wedderburn, Robin Wedderburn and Sue Wilmot.

Contents

Prologue - Stories and Truths 7

Part 1: Greek Myths

1 Arrogance (Theseus) 15
2 Regret (Daedalus) 19
3 Loneliness (Orpheus and Eurydice) 25
4 Revenge (Medea and Jason) 31
5 Loyalty (Alcestis) 37
6 Infidelity (Helen and Paris) 41
7 Blindness (Oedipus) 47
8 Determination (Creon and Antigone) 53
9 Envy (Midas) 59

Part 2: Greek Literature and History

10 Guile (Rhampsinitus and the Thief) 67
11 Vulnerability (Croesus and Sardis) 71
12 Courage (Plataea) 75
13 Haste (The Athenian Assembly) 81
14 Disunity (The Athenian Generals) 87
15 Captivity (The Athenian Soldiers) 95
16 Carelessness (The Athenian Fleet) 99
17 Death (Socrates and the Poisoned Cup) 105
18 Enlightenment (Plato's Cave) 113
19 Fear (The Sword of Damocles) 121
20 Bereavement (A Poem of Callimachus) 125

Part 3: Latin Literature and Roman History

21 Training (Hannibal) 135
22 Pride (Cicero) 141
23 Pleasure (Horace and Epicureanism) 145
24 Achievement (Horace and Poetry) 151
25 Sadness (Virgil and Life) 155
26 Conscience (The Emperor Nero) 161
27 Superstition (Pliny and Regulus) 167
28 Triviality (Pliny and the Roman Day) 173
29 Sleep (A Poem of Statius) 179
30 Terror (Domitian's Dinner Party) 187
31 Eternity (Hadrian's Farewell Poem) 193

Epilogue - Divinity 199

Appendix 1 - List of Greek and Roman Authors 211
Appendix 2 - Maps of Greece and Italy 217

Prologue

STORIES AND TRUTHS

∼

The Greeks and the Romans have passed down some wonderful stories to us. Their myths, history and literature have been a big part of my life since the age of seven, when I discovered an article on the Trojan War in a Children's Encyclopedia. This book draws on that wealth of material, exploring their views on life and then comparing their conclusions with the teachings of the Bible.

Why look to those ancient Classical writers for anything more than interesting stories? They are indeed interesting: one person who read some of the following chapters in draft was fascinated, much to her surprise. But many stories also have a moral (like the fables of Aesop). Literature invites us to think about life, and we can learn so many lessons from history.

And why the Bible? For many people it is a closed book, only ever read in RE lessons at school long ago. Perhaps they are making assumptions based on the Bible being ancient and irrelevant: admittedly it comes from a time and a culture very different from our own. But something is not necessarily useless and unimportant just because it was written in the distant past. "Do not murder", "Do not steal", "The love of money is a root of all kinds of evil", "Don't be anxious about the future" – principles like these do not have a Best Before date.

The Bible is roughly contemporary with Classical literature. The one extends from the Books of Moses (who led the Israelites out of slavery in Egypt in about 1270 BC) through to Saint John's Revelation (probably written about 90-100 AD), while the other covers the period from the Trojan War (about 1200 BC) through to the first two or three centuries of the Roman Empire.

The Greeks, Romans, Jews and Christians all wrestled with the deep questions of life, death and the universe. Sometimes they came to very similar conclusions; sometimes they diverged. This book sets out to compare the ancient truths of the Classical and the Biblical writers. I hope too that it will be an eye-opener for any readers who are new to the Classical World or the Bible and would like to know more.

Chapters 1-9 take Greek myths as their starting point. Chapters 10-20 draw on Greek literature and incidents from Greek history. Chapters 21-31 look at Latin literature and Roman history. The 31 chapters (daily reading for a month?) can be taken in any order. There is also an epilogue: this seeks to draw all the threads together and sum up the critical differences between Christianity and the Classical world.

***

I will add a brief word about how the Greeks and Romans have influenced our language and our thinking. For those who regard the Classical world as being very remote from our own, consider the following.

Expressions

Many words and sayings in English come from the Greeks or the Romans.

- An "odyssey" harks back to Odysseus and his long journey returning to Greece after the Trojan War.

- Your "Achilles heel" is your one weak spot: this too comes from the Trojan War period. Achilles' mother, the sea-nymph Thetis, had dipped him in the River Styx (one of the rivers of the Underworld) as a baby to make him invulnerable; but she had held him by the heel, which was the one place where he could be fatally wounded.

- "Greek gifts" are ones you cannot trust: the Trojans failed to realise that the enormous wooden horse left on their shore was not an offering to the gods but full of armed men.

- A "marathon" is a race that harks back to 490 BC, when the Greeks defeated the Persians as they were disembarking in the Bay of Marathon: following the battle a runner called Pheidippides ran back to Athens just over 26 miles away to announce the victory.

- "Herculean labours" remind us of the twelve hard tasks that Hercules had to perform to atone for a crime he had unwittingly committed.

- A "Pyrrhic victory" is named after the Greek King Pyrrhus who defeated the Roman army around 276 BC but lost far too many men in doing so.

- "Who will guard the guardians themselves?" (in Latin "Quis custodiet ipsos custodes?") comes in a satire of the Roman poet Juvenal: it is a perceptive warning about the need to check up on corrupt officials. There was an echo of Juvenal in Radio 4's Today programme on 21/4/21 when someone asked "Who is policing the police?"

Language

About half of English comes from Latin: many words (like permanent, status, momentum, agenda and propaganda) are actual Latin words, even if the meanings have developed over time. Or take the Greek prefix *para*. It was a preposition with various meanings including "beside" and "contrary to". We now see the same prefix in English words like parasol, parallel, paragraph, parapet and paratrooper. Ancient Greek has also given us *crisis* (the Greek word meaning judging), *climax* (meaning ladder), *comma* (cutting), *catastrophe* (overturning) and a host of other words. Many scientific terms come from the Classical languages, including the elements *neon* (literally "the new one"), *argon* ("the lazy one"), *krypton* ("the hidden one") and *xenon* ("the unfriendly one").

Life

The Greeks gave us the Olympic Games, which began in 776 BC. They gave us democracy, a system of government invented in Athens around 500 BC. They gave us the theatre, and some would argue that Greek drama of the 5th century BC has never been surpassed. And have the Romans ever done anything useful for us? Very much so - they gave us good roads, the arch, concrete, town planning, central heating and much else. Truly our debt to the Classical world is immense.

Part 1

GREEK MYTHS

Chapter 1

ARROGANCE

∽

Many legends surround Theseus. Born out of wedlock, slayer of many monsters, king of Athens, punished in the Underworld for the attempted carrying off of Persephone the wife of Pluto, rescued by Heracles, lost his throne, killed in exile – he was the mightiest of heroes. It was believed that he appeared to help the Athenians at the battle of Marathon, that decisive victory in 490 BC over the vast hordes of invading Persians. These were heroic exploits, but did his character match his deeds?

Aegeus the king of Athens visited Troezen in the Peloponnese (the southern part of Greece) and had an affair with Princess Aethra. He sailed away before Theseus was born, but he left a sword and sandals under a great rock. When Theseus was on the verge of manhood Aethra told him about this clue to the identity of his father, and the young Theseus strained his hardest to shift the rock and discover the secret. When at last he found the sword, his mother told him that his father was Aegeus; and Theseus immediately determined to go and make himself known to him. Picture the mother, reluctant to let go of her child, and the eager youth, setting out on his adventures and promising to return – the first of many promises that he forgot.

The Isthmus of Corinth is a narrow strip of land linking the Peloponnese to Athens and the rest of Greece. In those days the road was dangerous, and various monsters lurked there blocking the path of the unwary traveler. Theseus could have travelled by sea, which would have been safer, but he determined to go by the coast road and tackle these monsters. Among them were Sciron, who had a nasty habit of kicking his guests over the cliff; Procrustes with his famous bed (he tied guests to it, stretching them if they were too short for the bed and cutting off limbs if they were too long); and Sinis, a robber who killed travelers by bending pine trees down to the ground, tying his victims to the tops of the trees and then letting them spring up again. Theseus slaughtered them all, and he arrived in Athens with his reputation for strength and bravery firmly established. King Aegeus was getting old; yet as soon as he saw the sword, he acknowledged his son with joy and marked him out for his successor to the throne.

But there was a dark cloud on the horizon. Every year Athens had to send a tribute consisting of seven young men and seven maidens to King Minos of Crete, and these were to be thrown into the labyrinth and devoured by the Minotaur – that strange monster, half man and half bull. Much against his father's wishes, Theseus determined to go as one of the seven youths, trusting in his mighty strength. Fortune favoured him, for when he arrived in Crete the king's daughter Ariadne fell in love with him and determined to help him. She gave him a sword and a ball of thread. These enabled him to kill the Minotaur and get his fellow Athenians safely out of the many tortuous passages of the labyrinth. They fled by ship, and Theseus took Ariadne with him. However, what she thought was a marriage turned out to be just a convenient arrangement to help her arrogant "husband" on his path to further glory. They spent a night together on the island of Naxos, well to the north of Crete; but next morning Ariadne found that she was alone on the shore: Theseus had used her and then sailed away and abandoned her. (Happily, the god Dionysus saw her plight and rescued her: she became his wife and gave her name to a star. But that is another story and in no way justifies Theseus' behaviour towards her!)

Theseus and his party were approaching Athens. He had promised to put up a white sail if his mission had succeeded; and here was another promise that he broke, or just forgot. The anxious Aegeus, watching daily from the cliffs, saw a black sail approaching, and in despair he threw himself down into the sea below – the Aegean Sea, as it came to be known. So Theseus, the self-centred breaker of promises, became king of Athens. This was not the last of his adventures; but it shows most clearly his selfish and arrogant character.

Arrogance comes from the Latin word arrogantia; and my Latin dictionary translates that word as "an assuming, presumption, conceitedness…the proud, lordly bearing arising from a consciousness of real or supposed superiority, pride, haughtiness". This is poles apart from the ideal Christian character commended in the New Testament.

Jesus sets the example of humility. He washed the disciples' feet at the Last Supper (John 13.4-10). Earlier he had said "You know that those who are regarded as rulers of the Gentiles lord it over them, and their high officials exercise authority over them. Not so with you. Instead, whoever wants to become great among you must be your servant, and whoever wants to be first must be slave of all. For even the Son of Man did not come to be served, but to serve, and to give his life as a ransom for many" (Mark 10.42-45). Paul too commends this humble attitude: he says in one of his letters "Do nothing out of selfish ambition or vain conceit, but in humility consider others better than yourselves. Each of you should look not only to your own interests, but also to the interests of others. Your attitude should be the same as that of Christ Jesus". He continues by analysing the humility of Jesus, who took a succession of big steps down by becoming a human being, and then a servant, and then subject to death, even a shameful death on a cross (Philippians 2.3-11).

This humility is an attitude we need to cultivate. Peter wrote "Make every effort to add to your faith goodness; and to goodness, knowledge; and to knowledge, self-control; and to self-control, perseverance; and to perseverance, godliness; and to godliness, brotherly kindness; and to brotherly kindness, love" (2 Peter 1. 5-7). Peter makes it clear that it is up to us to seek these qualities; and it is obvious that one who holds on to an arrogant attitude will find it hard to attain them. True, the Holy Spirit helps us in our weakness, as he lives in the hearts of Christians and helps us become better people: "The fruit of the Spirit is love, joy, peace, patience, kindness, goodness, faithfulness, gentleness and self-control", says Paul (Galatians 5.22-23). These qualities are the very opposite of arrogance; but they don't come automatically. We have a part to play, since that fruit of the Spirit will not grow in us against our will.

Chapter 2

REGRET

~

Daedalus was a brilliant Athenian carpenter, sculptor, and inventor: his very name means *Cunning Craftsman*. Yet he fell far: his actions forced him into exile and he ended his life far away in Sicily, a broken man. How could such talent be matched by such personal failure?

Daedalus had a son called Icarus. He also had a nephew variously called Talus or Perdix, who came to work as his apprentice. Soon the nephew came to display or even surpass his uncle's skills. Perhaps it was jealousy, or the contrasting clumsiness of his own son, that caused Daedalus to do a terrible deed. Or was Talus' death, falling from the roof of the house, just an accident? Daedalus and Icarus had to flee from Athens, and they landed in Crete, many miles to the south. Here the craftsman was able to be of service to King Minos, who got him to build the famous labyrinth as a cage for a sinister monster. That monster was the Minotaur, a creature half bull and half human, the shameful offspring of Queen Pasiphae.

Minos was a cruel man. He feared that Daedalus knew too many secrets about him, and he imprisoned him and his son. But Daedalus escaped – not by land, for Crete was an island, and not by sea, for Minos had ensured that every single boat on the island was guarded. Instead, he built wings! The Roman poet Ovid (Metamorphoses VIII 189-235) describes this amazing invention and its dreadful consequences:

"He put feathers in order, starting with the smallest, a shorter one following a long one, such that you'd think they had grown on a slope... Then he bound the middle of the feathers with thread and the bottom of them with wax, and when they had been arranged thus he bent them with a gentle curve to imitate real birds. The boy Icarus was standing nearby. Not knowing that he was handling something so dangerous to himself, with smiling face at one time he chased the feathers blown by the wandering breeze, at another time he softened the yellow wax with his thumb; and with his games he was getting in the way of his father's amazing work.

After he had put the finishing touch to his task, the craftsman lifted his own body on the twin wings, suspended aloft by beating the air. He instructed his son and said "I advise you to take a middle course, Icarus, not too low, or the water will wet the feathers, and not too high, or the sun's fire will burn them. Fly between the two. Don't look at the stars, Bootes or the Great Bear or the drawn sword of Orion. Make your way following me." While giving these flying instructions, he fastened the strange wings to his son's shoulders. As he worked and gave advice, the old man's cheeks grew wet with tears and those fatherly hands trembled. He gave his son kisses that were destined never to be repeated. Then, rising on the wings, he flew ahead and feared for his companion, like a bird which has led out its tender offspring into the air from a high nest...

And now they had left behind the islands of Delos and Paros...At this point the boy began to delight in his bold flight; he deserted his leader and reaching for the sky he took too high a path. The proximity of the blazing sun softened the sweet-smelling wax which was the bond of the feathers. Suddenly the wax had all melted. He shook arms that were bare, and with no wings he had no purchase on the breezes. Crying out for his father, his mouth was covered by the blue waters, which thereafter took their name from him. But the unhappy father, now no longer a father, cried "Icarus! Icarus! Where are you? Where shall I look for you? Icarus!" he kept shouting. Then he saw the feathers on the waves, and he cursed his craftsmanship. He buried the body in a tomb, and the land was named after the one buried there."

Daedalus flew on, and he eventually ended up in Sicily. Here he made himself useful to King Cocalus, working on such projects as a reservoir, a steam bath and a fortress. However, Minos came in hot pursuit with a powerful force of ships. He demanded that the runaway craftsman and murderer should be handed over, and King Cocalus was forced to agree. But that night, as King Minos was taking a bath, legend has it that Daedalus suddenly released jets of boiling water onto him and killed him. Thus he saved his own life; but he could never save his own happiness. Those moments of madness when he had caused the deaths of his nephew and his son must have continued to haunt him till his dying day.

In the game of Chess the humble pawn has a unique feature. All the other pieces can move forwards or backwards, but the pawn, once it has moved forward, cannot retrace its step. So in life, some decisions we make can be reversed, some are hard to put right and some are irreversible. A word spoken in haste cannot be unsaid. An act rashly committed can lead to lasting damage. How do we cope, when we come to realise that we have made a mistake and cannot easily undo its effects?

The church in Corinth had made a mess of dealing with a particular situation: they had failed to put a check on the immoral behaviour of a member of the church. Then they came to their senses and acted to put matters right, to Paul's great relief. A bit later, in 2 Corinthians 7.8-10, Paul comments: "Even if I caused you sorrow by my letter, I do not regret it…your sorrow led you to repentance…Godly sorrow brings repentance that leads to salvation and leaves no regret, but worldly sorrow brings death."

Here Paul is describing two kinds of regret or grief or sorrow. There is worldly grief, where we regret what we have said or done, feel bad about it but do nothing to put it right; so the sense of regret just festers. Then there is a different sort of grief, godly grief, where we come to our senses, admit our mistake to God, put right anything we can and entrust the outcome to him. A simple prayer sincerely meant – "Lord, I'm sorry" – can transform the situation, or at the very least it can transform our feelings about it.

In a familiar story from Luke's Gospel (Luke 19.1-10), a corrupt tax collector called Zacchaeus was given the chance to change his ways: he resolved to give away half his goods to the poor and to make a fourfold repayment to anyone he had defrauded – and it changed his life. This man was able not only to admit his wrongdoing but also to make restoration, so any regret for his past actions would have been easier to deal with. Others in the Bible were not in that position – like Cain (who murdered his brother Abel), King David (who arranged for the death of Uriah in battle so that he could take Uriah's wife Bathsheba) and Judas (who betrayed Jesus to the Jewish authorities).[1]

---

1   See Genesis 4.1-16, 2 Samuel chapters 11 and 12, Matthew 27.3-5

All three were filled with regret and remorse afterwards. But only one truly repented: we can read David's heartfelt prayer of sorrow and confession in Psalm 51. A modern commentator writes "Here's one way to distinguish between worldly grief and godly grief: one mobilizes you into action, the other immobilizes you. Godly grief is a fruitful and effective emotion".[2] King David did not wallow in regret: he took action, repented, and thereby found a restored relationship with God.

---

[2] Kevin De Young in an excellent article entitled *Godly Grief, Worldly Grief* – see https://www.christianitytoday.com/pastors/2010/june-online-only/godly-grief-worldly-grief.html

Chapter 3

LONELINESS

One of the loneliest figures in Classical literature must be Orpheus returning from the Underworld. He was devastated because he had finally lost the person he went down to recover from Death's grip. But we have dived into the middle of the story…

Orpheus lived in Thrace, in northern Greece. Legend says that he was the son of one of the nine Muses, those goddesses who inspired music, poetry and literature. He had been given a lyre by the god Apollo and was a brilliant musician. He played so beautifully that everyone and everything stopped to listen. Even the rain came and the crops grew because of his playing.

And then he met Eurydice. Eurydice was a tree-nymph, but his playing enticed her out of her tree. They met, they fell in love, they married, and they were devoted to each other. Then came the dreadful day when Eurydice was walking in the woods and got bitten by a snake. Despite Orpheus' frantic efforts she died, and her soul took the sad, dark journey across the river Styx and down to Hades. Under this crushing blow Orpheus was a lost soul.

But someone urged him to go down to Hades to get her back. Surely his music could achieve anything, couldn't it? He went. He charmed Charon the Stygian ferryman with his lyre, crossed into Hades and approached the throne of Pluto, the king of the Underworld. Pluto was sitting on his throne, with his wife Persephone next to him. Orpheus played his heart out. The dark and dismal world of the dead had never heard such beautiful notes. Pluto was unmoved; but Persephone was deeply touched and begged her husband to give in to Orpheus' plea. At last he agreed. Orpheus could take his wife back to the world of the living, but there was a strict condition: he was not to look back at her till they had both reached the upper world.

Oh the agony of walking away! He steeled himself not to turn round and hardly dared to believe that the hard-hearted king had granted his request and that his wife really was following close behind him. They re-crossed the river; they climbed up towards the light; and then he could bear it no longer. He turned round – and she was lost to him forever. How nearly he had achieved his mission! How desolate, how grief-stricken, how utterly alone he was as he returned to his empty, joyless home.

Turning to the Biblical writers we find many examples of loneliness, and they illustrate this statement early in the book Genesis: "It is not good for the man to be alone. I will make a helper suitable for him" (Genesis 2.18). As God surveyed all the rest of his creation, he pronounced that it was good; but here was one thing that was not good. Adam was alone. He needed a suitable companion and helper, and shortly afterwards woman was created.

Some readers laugh at the idea of treating the opening chapters of Genesis as history; some see them as poetry which beautifully (but not literally) expresses important truths; others insist on the literal truth of every word. Whatever position we take in this debate, few can doubt that loneliness has been a factor in many people's lives all the way through history. Here are five examples taken from the Old and New Testaments.

Hannah cuts a sad and lonely figure in 1 Samuel chapter 1. Her husband Elkanah had two wives, and Hannah had no children, while her rival Peninnah had several. Peninnah gloated, and Hannah wept. One year in desperation, when the whole family had gone up to the house of the Lord at Shiloh, Hannah stayed on pouring out her heart silently to God. The priest Eli saw her lips moving and thought she must be drunk; but eventually he understood her bitterness and blessed her, and her prayers were answered with the birth of her son Samuel. Her isolation and loneliness must have been bitter indeed, till they were replaced by the joy of having a child.

Elijah was a powerful prophet in the days of the godless king of Israel, Ahab. He challenged the 450 prophets of the false god Baal to call down fire from heaven to burn up a sacrificed animal. They failed. Then Elijah prayed, and God answered with fire. It was a great victory, described in 1 Kings 18.16-40. Yet in the very next chapter we find Elijah exhausted, alone and thoroughly depressed. Queen Jezebel had heard of all that had happened to her favourite prophets; she had sent threatening messages, and Elijah had fled. Twice he complained to the Lord "I have been very zealous for the Lord God Almighty. The Israelites have rejected your covenant, broken down your altars, and put your prophets to death with the sword. I am the only one left, and now they are trying to kill me too". God's remedy included providing him with food, the chance to rest, and reassurance that there were seven thousand in Israel who had not bowed the knee to Baal. God also gave him three new tasks, one of which was to anoint Elisha as his successor. Elijah had certainly been suffering from loneliness – the feeling that he was utterly alone, everyone was against him, no one was on his side – but his fears were mis-placed, and God had been in ultimate control all along.

Jeremiah was another prophet who had a hard time standing alone against all the false prophets who prophesied "Peace, peace" to a king and a nation that had drifted far away from God. Eventually he was arrested and thrown into a well, and there he sank in the mire until a few faithful friends lowered ropes into the well to rescue him (Jeremiah 38.1-13). It is always easy to swim with the tide, and hard to declare God's message faithfully when you know it will incur isolation, unpopularity and violent opposition.

Paul too experienced loneliness at various times while on his travels, especially towards the end of his life when he was in prison. He writes to his young protégé Timothy "Do your best to come to me quickly, for Demas, because he loved this world, has deserted me and has gone to Thessalonica. Crescens has gone to Galatia, and Titus to Dalmatia. Only Luke is with me. Get Mark and bring him with you, because he is helpful to me in my ministry. I sent Tychicus to Ephesus. When you come, bring the cloak that I left with Carpus at Troas, and my scrolls, especially the parchments…At my first defence no one came to my support, but everyone deserted me. May it not be held against them. But the Lord stood at my side and gave me strength" (2 Timothy 4.9-17). We gather that Paul was cold, desperate for reading and writing materials, and only intermittently cheered up by Doctor Luke's visits. But though lonely, he was not totally alone or abandoned: he was conscious of God's presence and help. Perhaps he recalled encouragements from the Old Testament, like Psalm 46.1: "God is our refuge and strength, an ever-present help in trouble".

Jesus too was a lonely figure at times. In Mark 1.35 we read "Very early in the morning, while it was still dark, Jesus got up, left the house and went off to a solitary place, where he prayed". But this is different from the situations of Elijah, Jeremiah and Paul: he positively sought that lonely place, in order to be close to his Heavenly Father. Jesus also foresaw the loneliness of the Garden of Gethsemane, the betrayal by Judas, the trials before the Jewish and the Roman authorities, and the crucifixion: at the end of the Passover meal he said to his disciples "A time is coming, and has come, when you will be scattered, each to his own home. You will leave me all alone. Yet I am not alone, for my Father is with me" (John 16.32).

Is loneliness the same as being alone? The answer must be no, for some people deliberately seek and enjoy solitude, perhaps because it gives them the chance to think, or to pray, or to work at a particular project. In contrast, loneliness carries bad overtones and can often be painful.

Does everyone experience loneliness to the same degree? Again the answer must be no, for some people really enjoy their own company. At one end of life our understanding of autism has increased over the last few years: children on the autistic spectrum can seem to be happily absorbed in their own tasks and not to need interaction with others – often to the despair of their parents. At the other end of life it is sad to see the loneliness of so many old people isolated by deafness or dementia, maybe in a care home far away from any relatives. For many of this group solitude is unwelcome and painful.

How can we best cope with loneliness? Most of us need human company. But human company may fail us, and we need a relationship with God who never fails. Paul wrote in Philippians 4.4 "Rejoice in the Lord always. I will say it again: Rejoice!" There is no other key to lasting happiness, no other permanent antidote to loneliness. In the middle of the twentieth century there was a Rumanian pastor called Richard Wurmbrand, who suffered fourteen years of imprisonment under the

Communist regime, some of it in solitary confinement. It is hard to imagine how anyone could cope with such isolation, but he did. He even danced in prison (and the warders thought he had gone mad and rushed in with extra food!). When he was released and came home, he said to his wife "Before we kiss, I must say something. Don't think I've simply come from misery to happiness! I've come from the joy of being with Christ in prison to the joy of being with him in my family." [3]

---

3   https://www.persecutionblog.com/richard-wurmbrand/page/4/

Chapter 4

REVENGE

Jason and the Argonauts is probably one of the better-known stories from Greek mythology. Jason's father had been king of Iolcus (in Thessaly in Northern Greece). But he was deposed by his half-brother Pelias, and so Jason as an infant had to be whisked away from danger and brought up by the centaur Chiron. Later he came back to reclaim his kingdom. Pelias craftily agreed, provided Jason went off first to fetch the Golden Fleece. As Pelias knew well, this was virtually a suicide mission, since it was guarded by a never-sleeping dragon far away in the land of Colchis by the Black Sea. Jason gathered a team of heroes and set off in the newly built ship Argo. They had to row a long way, sometimes against strong currents, to reach their destination. To make matters more difficult, King Aeetes of Colchis was reluctant to let go of the Golden Fleece, and he first set Jason some almost impossible tasks – to yoke two fire-breathing oxen, plough a field with them, sow some dragon teeth and then deal with the armed men who promptly sprang up from the ground. However, the king's daughter Medea had fallen in love with Jason. She was a witch with magical powers, and she helped him to accomplish all these tasks and to get past the dragon that guarded his prize.

Jason and Medea sailed off together back to Greece; yet they did not live happily ever after. They had two children; but they failed to regain the throne of Iolcus and were driven away by Pelias' son Acastus. They settled in Corinth. There Jason began to grow tired of Medea. He wanted to marry Glauce, the daughter of Creon the king of Corinth: such a prestigious match to a local princess would no doubt further his ambitions for power and personal fulfilment.

Medea was devastated. She was also a dangerous person to treat in this offhand manner. Jason had been unfaithful after all that she had done for him – abandoning her father and her country, helping him to get the Golden Fleece and bearing him two sons. The 5th century BC dramatist Euripides explores her emotions in his play *Medea*. Here she addresses the chorus of Corinthian women:

> *"This unexpected blow that has fallen on me has destroyed my life. I am done for, I have lost all pleasure in life and I want to die, friends… Of all the creatures who live and have a brain, we women are the most wretched. First we need to pay out a vast amount of money to buy a husband – and to get a master for our bodies: this is piling evil on evil. And at this point the biggest question is, have we got a bad or a good husband? Divorce gets women a bad reputation; and denying a husband's demands is impossible…And when we have worked all this out, if our husband is happy to live with us and bear the marriage yoke, our life is enviable; if not, it's better to die. A man, when he is fed up with the company at home, goes out and puts an end to the tedium, turning to the company of friends or contemporaries. But we have got*

> *to have eyes for just one person. And they say that we live a life at home free of danger, while they face the battle and the spear. They're just so wrong! I'd rather stand in the battle-line shield to shield three times than give birth once…*
>
> *I am deserted, city-less, insulted by my husband, plundered from a foreign land, with no mother, no relative to extricate me from this predicament. So I make this request of you: if I can find a way to pay my husband back for these wrongs, keep quiet. A woman is generally full of fear and bad at facing the battle and cold steel. But when she is wronged in marriage, there is no foe more murderous."* (Euripides Medea 225-266)

And Medea does indeed come up with a scheme for revenge, a scheme which fully and comprehensively punishes all those who have wronged her. Jason is getting ready for his marriage to Princess Glauce, and Medea has been sentenced to exile. King Creon has unwisely given her 24 hours to prepare for her departure. She sends gifts via her children – a beautiful but poisoned robe and a coronet for the new bride. When Glauce puts them on, she dies in an agony of flames, as does her father who rushes up to try to help. Then Medea takes revenge to its extreme limit: she kills her own children, which is the one way to make Jason's misery complete. In the final scene of the play Jason rushes in to catch Glauce's murderer, only to see his children's lifeless bodies and Medea herself in a chariot drawn by dragons ready to make her escape to a new life in Athens. Thus Jason – foolish, unfaithful Jason – is left utterly alone. Medea's revenge is complete.

They say that revenge is a dish best served cold. Relish the careful planning, the precise execution and finally the glowing sense of achievement, as Medea did. But in her case it was costly, and she almost lost her nerve when it came to killing her own children. So, does revenge satisfy? Does it bring any sense of achievement? Does the achievement bring a feeling of closure and happiness?

Jesus said in the Sermon on the Mount "You have heard that it was said, "Eye for eye, and tooth for tooth". But I tell you, do not resist an evil person. If someone strikes you on the right cheek, turn to him the other also. And if someone wants to sue you and take your tunic, let him have your cloak as well" (Matthew 5.38-40). In other words he is saying we should not take revenge at all.

Some people misunderstand the "eye for eye" phrase. They know it comes from the Old Testament (in fact it comes at least three times, the first being Exodus 21.24), but they seem to have the impression that the words are encouraging a lashing out in uncontrolled revenge. They miss the subtlety of a punishment exactly matching the crime, neither too light (which is indulgent towards the perpetrator) nor too heavy (which is disproportionate to the offence). Revenge can often cause violence to escalate; and the Bible guards against this by giving us a progression in thinking. Before the Ten Commandments and the rest of the Mosaic Law revenge was unlimited; then Moses taught that the punishment should fit the crime – *only* an eye for an eye; and finally Jesus took the matter even further, forbidding any retaliation or revenge at all.

How then should we react when a person injures us or someone we love? Jesus said "Love your enemies and pray for those who persecute you" (Matthew 5.44). He gave the supreme example of this when he prayed for forgiveness for the soldiers who were nailing him to the cross (Luke 23.34). This is hard: no one is pretending that such readiness to forgive is easy. Yet there have been some startling examples of this forgiving attitude – notably a parent in Northern Ireland, Gordon Wilson, publicly forgiving the Provisional IRA bombers at Enniskillen who caused the death of his daughter Marie in 1987. Most of us have not (or not yet) had to face this awful question of whether we can forgive such a terrible deed. We can only read and wonder.

Chapter 5

LOYALTY

~

Loyalty is usually a quiet and self-effacing quality. While brashness, boldness and brilliance storm the heights and achieve great things, loyalty will probably stay quietly in the background and allow others to shine. We can learn a lesson from the various instruments in the orchestra: the easiest to play is your own trumpet, while the hardest is second fiddle!

The Athenian playwright Euripides was probably born in 484 BC and died in 406 BC. His life spanned the period when Athens was at its most powerful and drama was experiencing a golden age. In a male-dominated society he was particularly interested in the role and status of women, and many of his plays have a female central character.

Admetus was king of Pherae in northern Greece. He had a wife called Alcestis, after whom one of Euripides' plays is named. Death was claiming Admetus, but the god Apollo managed to get a concession out of the infernal god: Admetus would not have to die if he could find another to die in his place. He went round to all his family including his aged parents who were both still living; yet no one was willing to die in his place except Alcestis, who saw it as her duty as a wife and mother to render this service to her husband.

The final day came. There were tearful farewells. Admetus didn't know how he could cope and go on living without her, and he promised to remain faithful to her memory and not marry again. As he was making the final preparations for the funeral, the hero Heracles[4] arrived, hoping to stay with his old friend Admetus before continuing on a journey northward to Thrace. Admetus was obviously in mourning, but he concealed the identity of the deceased, merely saying that someone in the house had died, and that he would not dream of denying hospitality to his old friend. Heracles was escorted to the guest quarters and wined and dined lavishly. A servant, who had been ordered not to look gloomy despite the tragedy that had struck the household, was appalled at the guest's drunkenness. But when Heracles upbraided him for his sullenness, the truth at last emerged. Heracles was chastened, and he resolved to go to the grave and wrest Alcestis from the clutches of Death. He succeeded; and in the final scene he brought back a veiled woman, begging Admetus as a favour to look after her. Admetus slowly grasped the truth and welcomed her back with amazement and rejoicing.

Was Euripides saying that this is true loyalty, to be ready to die for those you love? Or was he poking the finger of criticism at men who would see nothing strange in valuing a man's life more highly than a woman's? Or was he just fascinated by a good story? Whatever the dramatist's purpose, the loyalty of Alcestis shines brightly.

---

4 The Roman name Hercules is probably more familiar; but Heracles is the Greek form of his name. He was a hero who was subsequently worshipped as a god.

At Remembrance Day ceremonies we often hear the words "Greater love has no-one than this, that he lay down his life for his friends". The words are fitting in the context of war. Some in the armed services may not have realised what they were letting themselves in for when they signed up, but others could clearly see the risks and the necessity of self-sacrifice. The original context of the words is the night before Jesus was crucified (John 15.13): he was pointing forward to his death the following day. At supper he had humbly washed the feet of the disciples. In the Garden of Gethsemane he had prayed that if possible the cup of suffering might be removed from him, but had submitted to his Father's will. As he suffered on the cross the chief priests mocked (Mark 15.31): "He saved others, but he can't save himself!" Little did they realise how true their words were. There was no other way to rescue fallen humanity: Jesus had to die in order to achieve his mission. It was an act of supreme loyalty to his Father and to mankind.

The Bible has many other examples of loyalty – that quiet dedication to the interests of others. There is the friendship between David and Jonathan, as described in 1 Samuel 20 and the following chapters. Jonathan was the son of Saul, the first king of Israel, who had drifted away from God and was going mad with jealousy over the rise of David. Jonathan could easily have taken his father's side and betrayed David, especially as he might have hoped to succeed Saul as king. But he could see his father's irrational behaviour and God's purposes for David and for the kingdom. He stayed loyal to David and helped him to escape from Saul's murderous intentions.

The final chapter in the book Proverbs has a description of the perfect wife: "A wife of noble character who can find? She is worth far more than rubies. Her husband has full confidence in her and lacks nothing of value" (Proverbs 31.10-11). The passage goes on to describe all she does for the household, the children, the servants and her husband. And who gets the glory? "Her husband is respected at the city gate, where he takes his seat among the elders of the land" (verse 23). As in the Greek world, so in Israel, male supremacy was the norm. But we have here another description of the ideal of loyalty.

At the end of his life Paul was in prison in Rome, and it was probably from there that he wrote his second letter to Timothy (which we also looked at in chapter 3). There is a sad picture of the aged apostle in the final paragraphs of the letter, abandoned by several of his friends and fellow workers. One of them is too much involved in worldly pursuits, while three others have gone off to important spheres of ministry. Luke is still with him, but he asks Timothy to join him as soon as possible, bringing with him Mark (probably the one who was later to write the second Gospel) and a cloak and some scrolls (2 Timothy 4.9-13). It is not often that we catch a glimpse of Paul at an unguarded moment. He is cold, in prison, nearly friendless and without books! But the bright spot is the loyalty of Luke, who has been his companion on many of his travels round the Mediterranean world and has not forsaken him even in that dark hour.

Loyalty is a wonderful quality. It seldom gets a mention in the newspapers, it doesn't mature quickly, but it makes the world a better place. We will allow King Solomon (in Proverbs 3.3 RSV) to have the last word: "Let not loyalty and faithfulness forsake you; bind them about your neck, write them on the tablet of your heart".

Chapter 6

INFIDELITY

~

"Was this the face that launched a thousand ships?" So wrote the Elizabethan playwright Christopher Marlowe about Helen of Troy. She was the most beautiful woman in the world and the wife of King Menelaus of Sparta (one of the leading cities in Greece). Then a Trojan prince called Paris came to their home, swept her off her feet and took her back to Troy. But once again we have dived into the middle of the story and need to start much further back.

Paris was the second son of King Priam of Troy and his Queen Hecuba. Before Paris was born, his mother had a dream that the child they were about to have would cause the destruction of their city. With great sadness they ordered a servant to take the infant out to the slopes of Mount Ida and leave him there to starve to death; and they consoled themselves as other children were born to them.

But Paris survived. He was brought up by a shepherd far from the city and became strong and athletic. One day he came to Troy, not knowing the facts of his birth. He took part in an athletic competition and beat everyone, including the princes of Troy. They were furious at the success of a mere peasant and ganged up on him – but he was saved by Princess Cassandra, who had the gift of prophecy and knew exactly who he was. So it came about that Paris was restored to his position as Prince of Troy. His parents forgot the dream, or they chose to ignore it; and in the course of time he was chosen as an ambassador to take a message to Sparta.

Stories can be like rivers with many tributaries. Only Paris knew of an event sometime before he returned to Troy, which was going to change the course of many lives. We must go back to a wedding banquet, the feast which celebrated the marriage of the sea-nymph Thetis to a noble mortal Peleus. (The issue of that union was the mighty warrior Achilles, but that is another branch of the story.) Eris the goddess of strife had not been invited to the wedding; but she came anyway, and she tossed into the midst of the feasting gods and goddesses a deadly gift. It was a golden apple, and on it was inscribed "For the fairest". Immediately all the goddesses claimed it, and squabbles broke out to spoil the happy occasion. It was so hard to decide between the leading contenders that Zeus the king of the gods proposed an ingenious solution. There was a lad on the mountainside near Troy who had been brought up far away from human company. He alone would be able to give an unbiased judgment.

The three leading goddesses Hera, Athene and Aphrodite duly appeared to a startled Paris. They gave him the golden apple, and they asked him to award it to the one who seemed to him the fairest and most beautiful. They promised lavish gifts. Hera the queen of the gods promised a great kingdom; the warrior goddess Athene promised great victories; and Aphrodite the goddess of love promised him the most beautiful woman in the world. Did Paris hesitate for even one second? He chose

Aphrodite and her gift; and the opportunity for the goddess to fulfil her promise came when Paris went to Sparta. There he was wined and dined by the king and queen; but when Menelaus was called away on some business, Paris could not let slip the opportunity. He wooed Helen. He persuaded her to elope with him to Troy. He took her back across the high seas. The Trojans were not pleased when Paris returned with his prize; but as Helen was so beautiful, they consented to fight for her if necessary.

And, of course, it was necessary. Menelaus was not going to ignore this insult, this theft, this violation of his hospitality. His brother was Agamemnon, the king of Mycenae and the most powerful king in Greece. Together they raised an army to sail across the Aegean Sea to Troy and recover Helen. This was the origin of the Trojan War, a ten-year struggle which the Greeks eventually brought to a successful conclusion by means of a trick, the wooden horse. They pretended to withdraw and sail away. They left the gigantic horse on the shore with armed Greeks inside it. The jubilant Trojans dragged the horse into their city, even making a breach in the city wall in order to do so. At dead of night the Greeks emerged from the horse; they caught the sleeping Trojans completely off their guard; and the city was captured and destroyed by fire. Such was the effect of Paris' adultery and Helen's infidelity.

There is much that could be said about adultery and infidelity – about the spiraling divorce rate in Britain in the twentieth century, the revolution in sexual ethics in the 1960s, and the Church of England's attempts to balance Biblical teaching on divorce against the need to understand and sympathise with human weakness and mistakes. However, thinking back to Paris' visit to Sparta, we will examine just one facet of this topic – how it all starts.

In the Old Testament the book Proverbs vividly portrays how easily young men fall into temptation, whether it is in the sphere of crime or drink or sexual immorality. The language of the book is old-fashioned, and it employs the balancing repetitions characteristic of Hebrew poetry. But the teaching is right up to date: if we choose the company of lawbreakers, excessive drinkers or adulterers, we shall in the end only be harming ourselves. Here are three passages on the subject of sexual immorality which are worth quoting at length:

- "Wisdom will save you from the ways of wicked men…it will also save you from the adulteress, from the wayward wife with her seductive words, who has left the partner of her youth and ignored the covenant she made before God. For her house leads down to death and her paths to the spirits of the dead. None who go to her return or attain the paths of life." (Proverbs 2.12-19)

- "For the lips of an adulteress drip honey, and her speech is smoother than oil, but in the end she is bitter as gall, sharp as a double-edged sword. Her feet go down to death; her steps lead straight to the grave…Now then, my sons, listen to me; do not turn aside from what I say, keep to a path far from her, do not go near the door of her house, lest you give your best strength to others and your years to one who is cruel…At the end of your life you will groan…You will say, "How I hated discipline! How my heart spurned correction! I would not obey my teachers…" Drink water from your own cistern…and may you rejoice in the wife of your youth." (Proverbs 5.3-18)

- "At the window of my house I looked out through the lattice, I saw among the simple, I noticed among the young men, a youth who lacked judgment. He was going down the street near her corner, walking along in the direction of her house at twilight, as the day was fading, as the dark of night set in. Then out came a woman to meet him, dressed like a prostitute with crafty intent...She took hold of him and kissed him and with a brazen face she said: "Come, let's drink deep of love till morning; let's enjoy ourselves with love! My husband is not at home; he has gone on a long journey..." With persuasive words she led him astray; she seduced him with her smooth talk. All at once he followed her like an ox going to the slaughter, like a deer stepping into a noose till an arrow pierces his liver, like a bird darting into a snare, little knowing it will cost him his life." (Proverbs 7.6-23)

That little phrase *all at once* is the final moment of decision. Up till that point he could still have said no. But he had made it hard for himself by deliberately walking down her street, and deliberately doing so at a particular time of day. He had walked into temptation, and it was by his own choice.

These scenes are described by a man (if indeed King Solomon was the writer or at least the editor of this book) and it is all from a male perspective. Who does he think is more to blame, the weak youth or the seductive lady? Some may think the finger of blame falls more heavily one way, some the other way; but it doesn't matter, for both are at fault. The same is true of King David's adultery with Bathsheba (discussed in chapter 7): David allowed his eyes and thoughts to wander, and Bathsheba provided the temptation.

Job is another Old Testament figure who sheds light on this topic. He suffered much affliction and loss – of his wealth, his flocks and his children. At a low point, he could still say "I made a covenant with my eyes not to look lustfully at a girl...If I have walked in falsehood or my foot has hurried after deceit... if my steps have turned from the path, if my heart has been led by my eyes, or if my hands have been defiled, then may others eat what I have sown, and may my crops be uprooted" (Job 31.1-8). When temptation comes, Job reminds us that the eyes can be the root of the problem.

This verdict ties in with Jesus' words in Matthew 5.27-28: "You have heard that it was said, "Do not commit adultery". But I tell you that anyone who looks at a woman lustfully has already committed adultery with her in his heart." These are stern words, setting what sounds like an impossibly high standard. But it will help us to recognise where it all starts and where it all leads – it starts with the eyes, and it leads to harm and destruction.

Chapter 7

BLINDNESS

∽

There are at least two sorts of blindness. There is physical blindness, and there is metaphorical, mental or spiritual blindness. Sometimes in Classical and Biblical literature there is an overlap between the two.

One of the most fascinating detective stories ever written is the story of Oedipus – a case of the detective striving to discover the murderer, totally unaware that he is the guilty one. His name is now linked with a particular complex in Freudian psychoanalysis – but we must go back to the ancient story as told by the 5th century BC dramatist Sophocles in his play *Oedipus the King*; and it is hard not to feel sorry for one whom fate treated so cruelly.

Oedipus was the son of Laius the king of Thebes (in central Greece) and his queen Jocasta. Before he was born, the Delphic Oracle warned Laius that if he had a son, that son would kill him. So the parents, in fear and with great sadness, ordered a servant to take the baby and leave him to die on Mount Cithaeron, not too far from Thebes, with a thong through his ankles. That might have been the end of the story, were it not that oracles have a nasty habit of coming true. The servant had pity on the baby, and instead of carrying out this horrible task he gave him to a shepherd from Corinth who happened to be pasturing his flock on the mountainside that summer. The shepherd took the baby home to his master Polybus the king of Corinth, who was childless. Polybus was very happy to adopt the baby. He gave him the name Oedipus, which means Swollen Foot, a legacy of that thong through his ankles.

The child grew to manhood. Then a servant at a banquet let slip a hint that he was not the genuine son of King Polybus. Puzzled and distressed, Oedipus went to consult the Delphic Oracle; but the only answer he got there was that he would kill his father and marry his mother. Horrified, he fled from the Oracle, determined to avoid Corinth and any contact with his supposed parents. He came to a place where three roads met. Coming the other way was a carriage with outriders, one of whom pushed Oedipus rudely into the ditch. Oedipus reacted strongly, whereupon the old man in the carriage leaned out and beat him with a walking stick. This was too much for Oedipus: he struck the old man and killed him outright, and he followed it up by attacking the outriders. Only one of these managed to escape.

Oedipus continued his journey and came to Thebes. He found the city in the grip of a plague inflicted by the Sphinx because they could not solve her riddle – "What goes on four legs in the morning, two in the afternoon and three in the evening?" He knew the answer – Man. At a stroke he had delivered the city from the Sphinx and her plague. The city rejoiced. They feted Oedipus, made him king and insisted he marry the recently widowed Queen Jocasta. That union produced four children, but then terrible consequences followed in the form of another plague; and that is the starting point for Sophocles' play.

In this crisis Oedipus sent his brother-in-law Creon to Delphi to ask the Oracle what should be done. The answer came back that they should avenge the murder of Laius, the former king. Oedipus confidently proclaimed a curse on the murderers and promised to do his utmost to discover who had done the foul deed. Now the blind prophet Teiresias appeared at the king's summons: he came reluctantly, but at length, goaded by Oedipus, he revealed in riddling language the whole truth – that Oedipus was the murderer, that he didn't know with whom he was living, that he was both father and brother to his children, and that he would be blind when he eventually left Thebes. Oedipus was furious, and even thought Creon had put Teiresias up to these slanderous accusations. Oedipus and Creon were shouting at each other when Jocasta appeared, calmed them down, and said that you can't really believe in oracles: Laius was not killed by his son but by robbers at a place where three roads met.

This was the phrase that caused the first pang of worry in Oedipus: was he the murderer of Laius, and should all those curses he pronounced on the murderers now rest on his own shoulders?

A messenger came from Corinth with news that Polybus was dead, and that the Corinthians wanted to crown him as their new king. Oedipus was grieved, but relieved that there was no danger now of him killing the man he thought of as his father – though he still feared the other part of the oracle concerning his mother. The Corinthian messenger noticed his grief and told him he need have no fear on that score, as he wasn't the son of Polybus anyway: the messenger had been shepherding sheep on Mount Cithaeron many years before and had received Oedipus as a baby – from one of Laius' servants – and given him to King Polybus to bring up as his own son. Jocasta, listening to all this, immediately grasped the truth and in terror begged Oedipus to explore no more; but Oedipus was determined to find the truth and summoned the servant who had met the Corinthian shepherd on the mountainside all those years ago. He came, very reluctantly, and the whole truth was revealed: it was the son of Laius and Jocasta, Oedipus with the swollen ankles, who had been destined for exposure on the mountain but had then been given to the Corinthian shepherd and brought up as Polybus' son; it was his own father whom Oedipus had killed on the road; and it was his own mother whom he had married after assuming the kingship of Thebes. In horror he blinded himself, and left Thebes a broken man. The detective had unmasked his own guilt. Once he had eyes but could not see the truth: now he was blind but knew it all.

The Bible often talks about blindness. Looking at the Old Testament, David was Israel's greatest king. He succeeded the first king, Saul, and enjoyed God's favour all through his life. As a lad he shepherded his father's sheep and got the upper hand against bears and lions. As a youth he slew the Philistine giant Goliath. As king his victories were celebrated by Israel. But then he fell from grace: he committed adultery with Bathsheba while her husband was away on military service. He tried to cover up the resulting pregnancy by ordering that her husband Uriah would be put in the front line at the hottest point of the battle. Uriah was killed, and David took Bathsheba. But then came the prophet Nathan, telling a simple story of a rich man who needed to provide a meal for a visitor. The rich man spared his own flocks and instead stole a poor man's one lamb. David, still blind to his own faults, was outraged. It wasn't till Nathan uttered the ominous sentence "You are the man!" that he came to his senses, repented, and found a restored relationship with God (2 Samuel chapters 11-12).

Turning to the New Testament, Jesus healed a blind man called Bartimaeus (Mark 10.46-52) and a man who had been blind from birth (John chapter 9). In this second case the disciples assumed it must be a punishment for his own sins or the sins of his parents. Jesus denied it, saying "This happened so that the work of God might be displayed in his life". After he healed him, the Pharisees confronted the man and questioned both him and his parents. They desperately tried to show that no miracle had taken place, but he stuck to his story with the memorable words "One thing I do know. I was blind, but now I see."

John Newton, the converted slave-trader, was probably thinking of this story when he wrote the words of the hymn Amazing Grace: "I once was lost, but now am found, was blind, but now I see."

We have moved from physical to spiritual blindness, which is exactly what happens at the end of John chapter 9: Jesus said "For judgment I have come into this world, so that the blind will see and those who see will become blind." Some Pharisees overheard him and asked "What? Are we blind too?" and Jesus answered "If you were blind, you would not be guilty of sin; but now that you claim you can see, your guilt remains." Those who know their need and come humbly to the Lord will find healing and help; while those who are boastful and claim to be able to see clearly are the ones who are inwardly blind but do not know it. What is worse is that they are deceiving not only themselves but others too: elsewhere Jesus said of the Pharisees "Leave them; they are blind guides. If a blind man leads a blind man, both will fall into a pit" (Matthew 15.14).

The same ignorance is found in the church at Laodicea. This was one of the churches in the Roman province of Asia to which John was instructed to send a letter.[5] "You say, I am

---

5 See the seven letters in Revelation chapters 2-3. The letter to Laodicea is in Revelation 3.14-22.

rich; I have acquired wealth and do not need a thing. But you do not realise that you are wretched, pitiable, poor, blind and naked." Laodicea was famous for its special eye salve – but spiritually it was blind. It prided itself on its trade and wealth – but spiritually it was poor.

And there lies the challenge. "Know yourself" was a motto inscribed in the forecourt of the temple of Apollo at Delphi, and the Biblical writers agree with that motto. Paul warns his readers (in 2 Corinthians 4.4) "The god of this age has blinded the minds of unbelievers, so that they cannot see the light of the gospel of the glory of Christ". Many people in the world are blind to spiritual truths; and like Oedipus, they are totally unaware of their blindness.

Chapter 8

DETERMINATION
~

What is the difference between determination and stubbornness? Is the first a good quality and the second bad? Or do they shade into each other, as the two main characters in Sophocles' play *Antigone* suggest?

It's the Oedipus family again. When that unhappy man had blinded himself, left Thebes to go into exile and finally found a peaceful conclusion to his life in a village near Athens, he left behind four troubled children. Their uncle Creon ruled Thebes; but Oedipus' sons Eteocles and Polynices were quarrelling over the kingship. Polynices attacked Thebes to reclaim his throne, while Eteocles defended the city. Both died in the ensuing battle, and Creon issued a decree that the patriot would receive an honourable funeral, while the traitor would be left unburied where he fell.

That left just the two girls. Antigone urged her sister Ismene to help her in burying the body of their brother Polynices. When Ismene shrank back from the idea, Antigone determined to act alone. Before any guards could be posted she went and scattered earth on the corpse. The guards in shame reported this to Creon. The earth was dusted off, and the guards kept watch with special vigilance. But there was a sandstorm, and after it cleared, they saw Antigone attending yet again to the burying of the body. When they brought her to Creon, she made no attempt to conceal what she had done. He appealed to the law of the land – his decree forbidding the burial of the traitor. She appealed to a higher law – the divine law that all dead bodies must be buried and that it was right and necessary for her to fulfil this obligation to her brother. In fury Creon ordered that she be walled up in a rocky tomb. A little food and water would be given her so that they could avoid the stigma of bloodshed, but she would soon starve to death.

Creon's son Haimon was engaged to Antigone, and he was also in touch with what the ordinary citizens were saying about the savage punishment of such a young woman. For these reasons he begged his father to think again; yet Creon refused to change his mind. The sentence was duly carried out. Then the blind prophet Teiresias came, and his dire warnings eventually persuaded Creon to relent. They went to the tomb to release Antigone; but alas, they were too late, for Antigone had hung herself. Haimon rushed at his father to kill him, and when the attendants restrained him, he turned the sword on himself. Creon's wife too, distraught at the deaths of Antigone and her son, perished by her own hand. At the end of the play Creon – stubborn Creon – was left utterly alone, a broken man.

Antigone had been determined to do what she thought was right and to obey divine law. Creon too had been determined to uphold the law of the land. In a sense both were in the right; and yet there were three needless deaths thanks to two people's stubbornness.

DETERMINATION

There are numerous examples of stubbornness in the Old Testament.

- Psalm 95 offers wise advice: "Today, if you hear his voice, do not harden your hearts as you did at Meribah, as you did that day at Massah in the desert…". This refers to an occasion a few days after the Israelites were rescued from Egypt: despite the extraordinary miracle of passing safely through the Red Sea, they started complaining about the lack of water and food and wanted to return to Egypt (Exodus 17.1-7).

- There is also a stark warning in Proverbs 29.1: "A man who remains stiff-necked after many rebukes will suddenly be destroyed – without remedy". Alas, we are often too proud or too obsessed with our own rightness to change our thinking. We maintain our resolve even in the face of God's word, or our conscience, or a mountain of adverse circumstances.

- Cain brought an offering of grain to the Lord (Genesis chapter 4) and was bitterly disappointed when his brother Abel's offering was accepted while his own was rejected. The account doesn't make it clear exactly why it was rejected: perhaps he didn't offer it in the right spirit of humility, as his reaction suggests. But whatever the reason, instead of quietly thinking through the rejection and changing his ways, he allowed his anger to fester until it led to the first murder in the Bible.

- Pharaoh was the ruler of Egypt when Moses approached him and requested that the Israelites be allowed to leave Egypt. He refused, and he kept on refusing despite the series of plagues that the Lord inflicted on his country. Each time a new catastrophe fell on them it looked as though he would give way; but when it abated, he hardened his heart once more until the very last and devastating plague, the slaying of the first-born throughout the land. Even then, having at last permitted the Israelites to depart, he soon changed his mind and pursued them as far as the Red Sea, with further disastrous consequences for his own army (Exodus chapters 5-14).

- Balaam was a prophet. Balak the king of Moab was worried about the advancing and all-conquering Israelite army and sent messengers asking Balaam to come and put a curse on the Israelites. Balaam prayed for guidance, and next morning gave a clear answer: "Go back to your own country, for the Lord has refused to let me go with you." Balak pressed him, and eventually he agreed to go. But on the way an angel with a drawn sword blocked their way. The donkey on which Balaam was riding saw the angel and turned off into a field. Balaam beat the donkey. The angel blocked their way again. The donkey tried to avoid the angel by pressing against the wall at the side of the path, and again Balaam beat the donkey. For the third time the angel blocked a narrow path, and the donkey could do nothing but lie down, only to receive a third beating from his master. Then the Lord enabled the donkey to speak: "What have I done to you to make you beat me these three times?" Finally God opened Balaam's eyes to see the angel, and so to realise that his disobedience and his stubbornness had almost cost him his life. Now truly humbled, he continued his journey and – to King Balak's annoyance – pronounced God's blessing on the armies of Israel. (See Numbers chapters 22-24)

DETERMINATION

- Hophni and Phinehas were the sons of the old priest Eli, and their story is told in 1 Samuel chapters 2-4. Eli had been a good mentor for the boy Samuel as he grew up serving the Lord at the Tent of Meeting at Shiloh. But he was less successful in guiding his own sons. They were worthless priests; they abused the sacrifices, helping themselves to the best portions of the meat being offered on the altar; and they slept with the women who served at the sanctuary. Eli rebuked them in vain, and eventually they were both killed in battle.

Turning to the New Testament, the Pharisees and other Jewish leaders showed an extraordinary blindness and stubbornness in the face of the miracles and the teaching of Jesus. He describes them several times as "blind guides" (for example in Matthew 23.16 and 24), and he directs a remarkable parable against them in Luke chapter 20.1-19. It is about a man who plants a vineyard and lets it out to tenants. At harvest time he sends a servant to collect some fruit as rent, but they beat him and drive him away. They treat subsequent messengers with similar violence, and when the owner sends his own son, they kill him. What will the owner do then? He will punish them appropriately and let out the vineyard to other tenants. The Jewish leaders knew that this story was directed against them; yet they still did not repent and acknowledge the authority of Jesus. Their stubbornness took the form of clinging on to their own power, position and rightness.

Ananias and Sapphira make a brief and sad appearance in Acts chapter 5. After the birth of the Church on the Day of Pentecost the followers of Jesus felt it right to share all possessions in common. But Ananias, having sold some property, deliberately kept back part of the proceeds, and he offered the rest to the apostles as if it was the total sum gained from the sale. Peter, with supernatural insight, challenged him about lying to God – and he promptly collapsed and died. Later his wife Sapphira came in, and Peter challenged her too. There was the opportunity to repent and to acknowledge the error of her ways; but she didn't, and her stubbornness led to her immediate collapse and death.

Saul (who later got the name Paul) provides us with a story of stubbornness that was eventually overcome. He had witnessed the remarkable death by stoning of the first Christian martyr Stephen; and he then embarked on a crusade of hunting out and arresting Christians. But he had a life-changing encounter with God on his way from Jerusalem to Damascus. Three days of physical blindness gave him the chance to review his life and to emerge as an utterly different person – now the strongest and most determined advocate of the faith he had once sought to destroy, ready to face persecution, suffering, floggings, shipwrecks and even death in the service of his Master. Initially he was stubbornly opposed to the Church; but having changed sides, he became the perfect illustration of the right sort of stubbornness and determination.

Chapter 9

ENVY

～

The Midas touch – just think of it! Everything you touch will turn to gold! Limitless wealth, a glittering palace...what could possibly be better than that? Who will not admire you and envy you?

Such was the gift that Midas the king of Bromium in Macedonia (now Northern Greece) requested: he had done a favour to the god Dionysus, and in return he had been granted a wish. When Midas made his request, Dionysus warned him that it might be a dangerous gift; but Midas was adamant. Next morning he awoke, eager to try out his new power. And it worked! The table turned to gold, and so did the chairs, the plates, the cups and everything he touched. But then he wanted to enjoy the scent of a rose from his famous rose garden: alas, it immediately turned to gold. He wanted breakfast: there too he was thwarted as all the food he touched turned to gold before he could eat it. Terrified, he prayed to the god to take away the now unwanted gift. Dionysus, amused, told him to wash his hands in the river Pactolus. When he did so, gold seemed to stream from his hands; everything he had touched turned back from gold to its normal state; and ever thereafter the sands of that river sparkled with gold.

How do we react when we meet or read about people with fabulous wealth – or fame or success or any of those other attributes that seem so important and desirable? Envy is an area where the Classical and the Biblical writers came to very similar conclusions. They may well have reached those conclusions for different reasons; but Christians can agree wholeheartedly with the pronouncements of the Roman satirists Horace and Juvenal on this topic. Here is what Horace wrote:

"How does it come about, Maecenas, that no one lives contented with the lot that his rational powers or chance have apportioned him but praises those who follow different paths? "Oh lucky merchants!" says the elderly soldier whose body is now broken by much hard toil. The merchant on the other hand, when the south winds are battering his ship, says "The soldier's life is preferable! Why? You charge, and in one brief moment comes swift death or joyful victory". The man who is skilled in justice and the laws praises the farmer when a client beats at his door around cockcrow. The other, who has given a pledge and been dragged away from the countryside to the city, proclaims that the only happy people are those who live in the city..." (Horace Satires 1.1) The grass is always greener on the other side of the fence, says Horace. Little do we realise that those we envy may not be as carefree as we think: they may actually envy us.

Juvenal writes in a similar vein: *"In all the lands which stretch from Gades [Gibraltar] to the east and the river Ganges, few people are able to shake off the cloud of error and distinguish between real benefits and their opposites. What do we fear or desire rationally? What do you desire so sensibly that you don't regret the attempt and the prayer when it has been answered? People in both civilian and military life ask for things that will actually harm them. Eloquence –*

the gift of the gab – has been the death of many. One died through trusting in his strength and his much-admired muscles. But more are strangled by money piled up with excessive care..." (Juvenal Satire 10). Juvenal was thinking particularly of the two greatest orators of the Ancient World, the Athenian Demosthenes and the Roman Cicero, both of whom met violent ends; of Milo the strong man who found a tree trunk half split by a workman's wedges, tried to finish the job with his bare hands but only succeeded in dislodging the wedges, and then he got stuck and attacked by a wolf; and of Seneca, one of the richest men in Rome till he fell foul of his erstwhile tutee the emperor Nero.

Many centuries later Samuel Johnson imitated this satire of Juvenal and called it "The Vanity of Human Wishes": it is an apt title. Juvenal particularly spotlights wealth, political power, eloquence, military glory, long life and physical beauty as foolish things for which to pray; and near the end of the satire he offers these wise words: *"If you want advice, you will leave it to the gods themselves to give what suits us and is profitable for our situation...A man is dearer to them than he is to himself... One should pray for a healthy mind in a healthy body. Ask for a brave spirit, one with no fear of death...".* It is indeed wise to limit our wishes to "a healthy mind in a healthy body" (*mens sana in corpore sano*), and the phrase is still quoted today (in Latin!) nearly two thousand years after it was written.

There are surprising echoes of Christian language all the way through these passages:

No one lives contented... "I have learned the secret of being content in any and every situation, whether well fed or hungry, whether living in plenty or in want" (Paul in Philippians 4.12 – and he was in prison at the time). A similar lesson in contentment comes in Hebrews 13.5-6: "Keep your lives free from the love of money and be content with what you have, because God has said, Never will I leave you; never will I forsake you.

So we say with confidence, The Lord is my helper; I will not be afraid. What can man do to me?"

People ask for things that will actually harm them... "You want something but don't get it. You kill and covet, but you cannot have what you want. You quarrel and fight. You do not have, because you do not ask God. When you ask, you do not receive, because you ask with wrong motives, that you may spend what you get on your pleasures" (James 4.2-3); "People who want to get rich fall into temptation and a trap and into many foolish and harmful desires that plunge men into ruin and destruction. For the love of money is a root of all kinds of evil..." (1 Timothy 6.9-10).

But more are strangled by money... "Give me neither poverty nor riches, but give me only my daily bread. Otherwise, I may have too much and disown you and say, Who is the Lord? Or I may become poor and steal, and so dishonor the name of my God" (Proverbs 30.8-9).

Leave it to the gods themselves to give what suits us... "Your Father knows what you need before you ask him" (Matthew 6.8).

A man is dearer to them [the gods] than he is to himself... "I have loved you with an everlasting love"; "Whoever touches you touches the apple of his eye"; "As a father has compassion on his children, so the Lord has compassion on those who fear him"; "Because of the Lord's great love we are not consumed, for his compassions never fail"; "God so loved the world that he gave his one and only Son"; "God is love". (Jeremiah 31.3; Zechariah 2.8; Psalm 103.13; Lamentations 3.22; John 3.16; 1 John 4.8).

Ask for a brave spirit, one with no fear of death... "For to me, to live is Christ, and to die is gain" (Paul in Philippians 1.21); "Do not be afraid of those who kill the body but cannot kill the soul. Rather, be afraid of the One who can destroy both soul and body in hell" (the words of Jesus in Matthew 10.28).

Is there then a difference between the Classical and the Biblical writers? In both we find the conclusion that we should not seek to amass possessions but live simply and with contentment. Perhaps it is only in the source of the teaching that we can discern a difference. Horace and Juvenal appeal to reason and argue gently and humorously (in the case of Horace) or vehemently and angrily (in the case of Juvenal) for these truths. In the Bible we find a simple and clear command, "You shall not covet..." (Exodus 20.17), given by a loving and wise God who knows what is truly best for us.

Part 2

GREEK LITERATURE AND HISTORY

Chapter 10

GUILE

~

Way back in the mists of time in Ancient Egypt a story was told of a king called Rhampsinitus. It may be wholly or partly fictitious, but Herodotus the Greek historian, sometimes called the father of History, could never resist a good story (Herodotus *Histories* 2.121).

Rhampsinitus was incredibly rich, and he got a craftsman to build a special treasure chamber. But the craftsman was dishonest and had secretly built in a removable stone. On his deathbed he told his two sons about it; and they immediately started removing treasure, in small amounts at first to lower the chances of detection.

The king eventually noticed that treasure was missing even though the seals and locks on the door were intact. So he set a trap. The next time the brothers entered the treasure chamber, one of them got caught in the shackles and realised he was unable to escape. He begged his brother to cut off his head and remove it, so that at least one of them would avoid capture. Next morning the king found the headless corpse and wondered what on earth he could do. He decided to hang the body in the public square with guards stationed nearby to arrest anyone who gave any signs of recognising or reacting to the corpse. In this way the mother of the two thieves discovered the truth, and she threatened her remaining son that she would denounce him to the king if he did not recover the body. His pleas to her fell on deaf ears, and he was at his wits' end.

Suddenly he had an inspiration. He loaded a train of donkeys with wineskins, and as he was entering the square, he undid some of the skins so that a little of the wine started escaping. Then he pretended to kick up a great fuss and beat the donkeys. The guards came rushing up to help. At first he pretended to push them away, but then he accepted their assistance and even offered them a wineskin to show his gratitude. And then another. And another. Eventually they were totally drunk and slept at their post while he removed the body of his brother under cover of darkness.

Yet again the king was perplexed. But he had one more trick up his sleeve. Some may find the last part of this story hilarious, some may find it distasteful, and some may say it removes any possible doubt about whether the whole story is fact or fiction. The king instructed his daughter to go down to the local brothel and to ask each of her clients what was the worst thing they had ever done: if anyone boasted about the theft of the treasure and the corpse, she was to grab hold of him and call the guards stationed nearby. The thief came, but he smelt a rat and had already provided himself with a false arm from a corpse. She innocently asked her question, he told her all about the thefts, she grabbed him – but it was the false arm, and he escaped. Rhampsinitus now felt he had been truly outwitted and would never be able to arrest the thief; so he proclaimed an amnesty and his daughter's hand in marriage if the thief would come forward. He did, he claimed his reward, and the story ended happily.

If that was a strange story from the Classical world, here is an equally strange parable in Luke chapter 16. A dishonest manager is accused of wasting his master's goods and is about to appear before him to give a full account. He wonders what he can do, given that he is probably about to lose his job and doesn't feel up to either manual work or begging. Then he hits on a cunning plan: he calls in his master's debtors and encourages them to falsify the amounts on their bills. "How much do you owe? 800 gallons of olive oil? Take your bill and make it 400!" His purpose was to ensure he would be welcomed into those debtors' houses when he was unemployed and destitute. And the remarkable feature of Jesus's story is that the master commended him!

Two tales of dishonest servants…robbing rich masters… in danger of discovery and punishment…but finding a cunning way of avoiding punishment and even gaining the rich man's favour…and the link between the two stories is guile, shrewdness, cunning.

We need to look closely at Jesus's explanation of the parable. "The master commended the dishonest manager because he had acted shrewdly. For the people of this world are more shrewd in dealing with their own kind than are the people of the light. I tell you, use worldly wealth to gain friends for yourselves, so that when it is gone, you will be welcomed into eternal dwellings." The first point is that the manager was commended for his shrewdness, not for his dishonesty. Jesus wants his followers to be wise, and that would include not being gullible and not being doormats, constantly downtrodden by others. Elsewhere (Matthew 10.16) he says "I am sending you out like sheep among wolves. Therefore be as shrewd as snakes and as innocent as doves."

Jesus takes this point further: he says that worldly people can be wiser than Christians in their day-to-day dealings.

Yes, Christians are children of light; yes, they see and know the truth, and their eternal destiny in heaven is secure – but unfortunately they are sometimes too naïve and unworldly.

How then should a Christian use worldly wealth? If we have been entrusted with it, one of the ways we can use it is to make friends – not so that they can repay our hospitality (like the dishonest manager), but so that they can thank us for our friendship and our sharing the gospel message with them when we arrive at the eternal dwellings. We need to exercise shrewdness – perhaps this is a better word than guile or cunning, both of which carry connotations of trickery and dishonesty. We need to use whatever riches and resources we have wisely and prayerfully during our earthly life.

Chapter 11

VULNERABILITY

~

Croesus was the king of Lydia in Asia Minor (now Turkey). He was fabulously wealthy, so much so that the phrase "as rich as Croesus" has passed into our own language. Various stories were told about him in ancient times, including one where he had a conversation with the Athenian philosopher Solon. Croesus was boasting to Solon about his wealth and asking him who was the happiest person in the world. He thought he knew the answer – himself – but Solon had other ideas about true happiness and mentioned two young Greeks from the city of Argos, Cleobis and Biton, who had won prizes for their athletic prowess and died young at the height of their fame.[6] Solon had also stressed that you should never count a man happy until he is dead: he may enjoy good fortune when young, but if he ends his life in poverty and misery, he cannot be reckoned as happy.

Cyrus the Great was king of the expanding Persian empire; and Croesus was not sure what to do about this threat on his

---

6 The full story, whether fact or fiction, is told in Herodotus 1.29-33.

eastern border. He wanted to consult the gods. But which of the oracles available in the Greek world could be trusted? He therefore devised a test. He sent out servants to various oracles with instructions to ask them this question on the hundredth day after their departure: "What is King Croesus doing at this precise moment?" In fact he was boiling some tortoise and lamb in a bronze pot, and the Oracle at Delphi described this rather unlikely operation perfectly. Now Croesus asked the Oracle the vital question: should he attack the Persian Empire? The Oracle gave the reply "If you cross the river Halys, you will destroy a great empire". The Halys was the boundary between Lydia and Persia, and Croesus, failing to observe the ambiguity in this response, ordered an attack on Persia. But alas, it was his own empire that was destroyed: Croesus and Cyrus met at the battle of Thymbra in 546 BC. Croesus was defeated and had to flee for refuge to his citadel Sardis. Here he thought he was safe, for the city was supposed to be impregnable.

Sardis did indeed have strong defences and high walls. But on one side the cliffs were so steep that the Lydians didn't see the need for much in the way of walls and armed patrols. Cyrus offered a great reward to anyone who could find a way into the city. One Persian soldier was looking at the seemingly precipitous cliffs when a Lydian soldier leaned over and accidentally dropped his helmet. But he didn't just shrug his shoulders and abandon it: he climbed down by a hitherto unseen path to retrieve it. That was the route by which the Persian soldiers were able to get into the city. The guards were overpowered and Croesus was captured.

Cyrus had intended to put Croesus to death, and an enormous pyre was built. As the flames rose higher, Croesus presumed his end was near and said aloud those words of Solon, that you should never count anyone happy until he is dead. The watching Cyrus was intrigued: he ordered the flames to be put out so that he could question Croesus further. Doubtless Herodotus has embellished the story at this point: a conveniently timed rainstorm was sent by Apollo, the god of the Delphic Oracle, and Croesus survived. [7]

Sardis was vulnerable in just one spot – an Achilles heel, you might say. But King Croesus also perfectly illustrates the vulnerability that comes from blindness to one's own faults. He trusted in his own wealth and cleverness, and he only came to his senses when it was almost too late.

Sardis in New Testament times was one of the seven churches of Asia to which the Apostle John was instructed to send a letter; and some of the phrases in that letter seem to hark back to the city's vulnerability and its capture by Cyrus: "I know your deeds, you have a reputation of being alive, but you are dead. Wake up! Strengthen what remains and is about to die, for I have not found your deeds complete in the sight of God. Remember, therefore, what you received and heard; obey it, and repent. But if you do not wake up, I will come like a thief, and you will not know at what time I will come to you" (Revelation 3.1-3). They were blind to their own faults; they were full of spiritual pride; but at any moment the Lord might come to them and find them unprepared – just as the soldiers of Cyrus had caught them off their guard many centuries earlier.

Laodicea was another of those seven churches and received a similar rebuke: "You say, I am rich; I have acquired wealth and do not need a thing. But you do not realise that you are wretched, pitiful, poor, blind and naked" (Revelation 3.17). Again, pride made them blind and therefore vulnerable.

Paul has some telling words for those who are vulnerable to pride and spiritual blindness: "So, if you think you are standing

---

[7] See Herodotus 1.46-55 (Croesus and Delphi) and 1.72-91 (Croesus and Cyrus).

firm, be careful that you don't fall!" (1 Corinthians 10.12). Our Achilles heel may be love of money, or sexual temptation, or craving worldly success, or occult involvement, or a host of other dangers. There is a lesson to learn from ancient Sardis: forewarned is forearmed.

We need to add a footnote: there is one sense in which vulnerability can be a positive quality. It is when we offer genuine openness, honesty and friendship to people. Paul was very honest about how low he felt when he first arrived in Corinth (1 Corinthians 2.1-3): "When I came to you, brothers, I did not come with eloquence or superior wisdom...I resolved to know nothing while I was with you except Jesus Christ and him crucified. I came to you in weakness and fear, and with much trembling." In a subsequent letter he writes of difficulties and pressures (2 Corinthians 1.8-9): "We do not want you to be uninformed, brothers, about the hardships we suffered in the province of Asia. We were under great pressure, far beyond our ability to endure, so that we despaired even of life...But this happened that we might not rely on ourselves but on God, who raises the dead." Paul is taking a risk when he speaks so frankly and honestly about his feelings and his weakness: his readers might easily have reacted by despising him and looking elsewhere for stronger leaders. But his vulnerability unlocked a response in his readers; and today it gives a ring of authenticity to his preaching and his writing.

Chapter 12

COURAGE

~

Courage is often associated with fighting against the odds. It is easy to be bold when you have superior forces, but much harder when you are the weaker side facing the stronger, a David facing a Goliath.

The name Thermopylae may once have been unfamiliar to many, but in 2007 the film "300" helped to put it on the map. The film tells the story of those courageous 300 Spartans who held back the vastly superior numbers of the invading Persian army in 480 BC. Or rather, it is based on that story: film-makers don't always worry about historical accuracy! Why can't they stick to the original account in the Greek historian Herodotus? But he too almost certainly embellished the bare bones of the story.

The Spartans and a few allies had marched northwards to hold the narrow pass at Thermopylae in central Greece. Protected by the mountains on one side and the sea on the other, they beat off all the enemy attacks for several days, and the Persian King Xerxes became more and more frustrated.

But then a Greek traitor showed the Persians a path over the mountains, enabling them to attack the defenders of the pass from the rear. Leonidas, the Spartan leader, was appalled; but he sent his Greek allies away, while he himself and the 300 Spartans fought to the bitter end and sold their lives dearly. Truly, the courage of those Spartans is legendary.

Less well known is the story of Plataea. And yet this would probably make an even better film, featuring a dastardly peacetime attack on a neighbouring city, a siege that was thwarted by the astonishing ingenuity of the defenders, and a well-planned but hair-raising escape over the enemy walls at dead of night. Thucydides, the Greek historian with an eye for accurate details, will be our guide.

Plataea was a small town in central Greece, not far from the Oracle at Delphi, and about eight miles from a powerful neighbour, Thebes. In 490 BC Plataea had been the only Greek state to send help to the Athenians when the vast forces of the Persians were disembarking in the bay of Marathon, just over 26 miles from Athens. The Spartans had a custom of not gathering their army together till the full moon, so they arrived too late. Other Greek states were too afraid. It was left to a small force of Athenians and Plataeans to charge down the hill at the Bay of Marathon and, against all the odds, to drive the disembarking Persians back into the sea. Ever thereafter the Athenians had a soft spot for little Plataea. (It was after this battle that a runner called Pheidippides ran back to Athens with news of the victory: he quite literally ran the first "marathon".)

Scene 1: The dastardly attack

Nearly sixty years later, in the spring of 431 BC, there were severe tensions between Athens and Sparta, the two leading cities in Greece. The Thebans were allies of Sparta, and for some time they had been looking for an opportunity to capture their annoying neighbour Plataea. The approach of war gave them the perfect opportunity. Very early one morning a small force of 300 Thebans managed to get into Plataea and terrify the inhabitants into surrendering.

However, the Plataeans soon realised that the Thebans were few in number and had not yet received reinforcements. So, while it was still dark, they made a sudden and successful counterattack, and the Thebans found themselves on the run in a city they did not know. Many were captured, and these hostages proved to be a useful bargaining tool when Theban reinforcements did eventually arrive. These reinforcements would have been a threat to the fields and farms outside Plataea, but they had to retreat ignominiously when they heard about the plight of the first Theban attacking party.

Scene 2: The siege

Soon after these events the long-expected war broke out between Athens and Sparta – the so-called Peloponnesian War (as Sparta was head of a coalition consisting mainly of the cities in the southern part of Greece, the Peloponnese). At first the Spartan army invaded the land round Athens every summer, and Athenians used their navy to make reprisal raids round the coast of the Peloponnese. But in the third year of the war there was a plague in Athens, so the Peloponnesian army diverted to Plataea at the request of the Thebans and started besieging it. The various phases of the siege are described in vivid detail by Thucydides (starting from book 2 chapter 2), and they illustrate the courage of the Plataeans in defending and then planning to escape from their city.

First the Peloponnesians built a wooden palisade round the city. Then they began work on a huge siege mound. It took seventy days or more to heap up earth, wood and stones; but the Plataeans countered this by raising the height of their own city wall. They also opened a gap in their wall and started removing the earth of the mound. Perceiving this, the Peloponnesians reinforced their mound with lumps of clay. Undeterred, the Plataeans dug a mine and started removing the earth of the mound from underneath, so that no matter how much the enemy put on top of the mound, it constantly sank down. They also built a new section of inner wall in the shape of a crescent, in case they needed a second line of defence. The Peloponnesians brought up siege engines; but the Plataeans used lassoes or dropped heavy beams to destroy them. Beginning to despair, the Peloponnesians tried fire. They heaped up faggots with sulphur and pitch against the city wall, and the resulting conflagration was so massive that it would have destroyed the whole city, had there not been a timely storm of rain. Eventually the besiegers gave up and decided to build a great wall round the city. The Athenians had long since taken the women and children to a place of safety, so just 400 Plataeans, 80 Athenians and 110 women bakers were cooped up inside.

Scene 3: The perilous escape

We move on about a year and a half, to the fourth winter of the war. The Plataeans were running out of supplies, and there seemed no hope of help from Athens, so they formed a daring escape plan. The wall encircling them actually consisted of two walls sixteen feet apart, with battlements and towers at intervals. First the Plataeans made scaling ladders: it wasn't easy to calculate the required length, but they got a pretty good idea by counting the layers of bricks in the enemy wall. Then they chose a dark and stormy night when the guards would be sheltering in the towers rather than patrolling the battlements. Over 200 men moved out, set up the ladders halfway between two towers, sent a small party of six men to each tower to deal with any guards who came out on patrol, and started to cross.

Then disaster struck. One of the Plataeans dislodged a tile, and the clattering alerted the nearest guards. However, the Plataeans immediately overpowered them, and then they used the towers to shoot arrows at the rest of the enemy. The Peloponnesians set off fire signals to get help from Thebes, but the Plataeans in the city immediately raised confusing counter signals. The Peloponnesians also had a special emergency force of 300 who rushed round to prevent the escape attempt, but the Plataeans in the city created a diversion by pretending to attack a different part of the wall. Amid the confusion, just one archer was caught while 212 Plataeans managed to get away. They set off first in the direction of Thebes, not Athens, and so were able to disappear into the hills and eventually reach safety.

Scene 4: The end of the story

The following summer, alas, those who had remained in the city were compelled by starvation to surrender, and the Peloponnesians put them on trial and dealt with them harshly. But nothing can detract from the ingenuity and courage displayed by the Plataeans, both in the defence of their city and in their audacious escape.

There are parallels here with first century AD Christianity, which was trying to survive and grow in a hostile environment. We read in Luke chapter 9 of Jesus sending out the twelve disciples in pairs to preach and to heal. His instructions were

"Take nothing for the journey – no staff, no bag, no bread, no money, no extra tunic…If people do not welcome you, shake the dust off your feet when you leave their town…". Perhaps it seems straightforward to our ears. But in effect Jesus was saying "You've seen me healing the sick and casting out demons. Now you go and do it!" Would it work? Would they be able to call on the same power that Jesus had used? It needed courage – faith to trust that they were not being sent out on a fool's errand, and that they would not be overwhelmed by any opposition. They obeyed, they went, they saw, and they were amazed. In the following chapter we read of seventy-two being sent out with similar instructions. Jesus warned them "Go! I am sending you out like lambs among wolves" (Luke 10.3), but they returned enthusiastically saying "Lord, even the demons submit to us in your name".

After all this success Peter lost his nerve on the night when Jesus was betrayed and arrested. To save his own skin he denied three times that he even knew Jesus. Yet he was restored and forgiven by Jesus after the Resurrection, and in the early chapters of Acts we read of him preaching boldly, first to the crowds on the Day of Pentecost (Acts 2) and then to the Jewish authorities following the healing of a crippled man (Acts 3 and 4). Ever since then, from the first to the twenty first century, Christians have been attacked, slandered, persecuted or murdered for their faith. Whenever they find themselves under attack and in the minority, they need the courage that David showed when facing Goliath (1 Samuel chapter 17); the confidence that Gideon showed when he surrounded the hordes of the Midianites with his force of just 300 men (Judges chapter 7); and the boldness that Peter and the other disciples displayed in the first century AD. And this courage comes from knowing God and trusting in his infinitely wise and loving purposes, whatever the danger, whatever the cost.

Chapter 13

HASTE

~

"More haste, less speed", says the well-known proverb. Haste sometimes leads to wasting time rather than saving time; sometimes it leads to disaster. If we are filling in a form hurriedly and with insufficient care, it is annoying (though not always disastrous) when the form is sent back to us for correction before it can be properly submitted. But a batsman in a test match, or a snooker champion in the deciding frame, needs patience: a mistake made in haste might throw away the whole game.

Ancient Athens invented democracy around 500 BC. While other Greek cities were ruled by kings, tyrants or oligarchies (where the city was ruled by the few, the elite), Athens gave the ultimate say to the assembly of citizens, and the very word *democracy* means *power of the people*. The system worked reasonably well for the first 70 years or so. Then in 431 BC came the great war between the two leading Greek cities Athens and Sparta. Athens had an empire based on sea-power. Sparta headed a league based on the power of the army. The Spartans started annual invasions of Athenian territory, ravaging the land and trying to provoke them to fight a pitched battle. The Athenian statesman Pericles advised them to hold firm behind their walls, and then do sea-borne raids of the Peloponnese – the southern part of the Greek mainland where Sparta and some of her allies were located. At first the Athenians followed the advice of Pericles; but he died in the third year of the war, and he was succeeded by a new class of political leaders who lacked the Periclean combination of wisdom, honesty and caution. Two episodes nicely illustrate the effect of this change.

In 427 BC Mytilene, the chief city on the island of Lesbos, revolted from Athens; but it was subdued with reasonable swiftness thanks to Athenian sea-power. The Athenian commander Paches sent messengers back to Athens for instructions on how the city should be punished; and the assembly in anger passed a decree that all the men should be put to death and the women and children enslaved. A boat was duly dispatched carrying these orders.

Next day there was a change of heart, and a feeling that they had done something too savage. A new assembly was summoned and the question was reopened – although it was technically illegal to go back on a decision of the assembly. A loud-mouthed demagogue called Cleon accused the democracy of being incapable of running an empire: if they let Mytilene off lightly now, in future every ally would be more likely to revolt, knowing that the consequences would not be fatal. A more cautious speaker, Diodotus, advised greater leniency: if they followed Cleon's way, every revolting city in the future would fight to the bitter end, knowing what would follow if they sought an honourable surrender. A new vote was taken. It was close, but the motion of Diodotus just carried the day, and another boat was sent off to countermand the previous instructions.

The bad news was that the first boat had a 24 hour start on its three-day journey across the Aegean Sea. The good news was that the crew were rowing slowly because of the horrid nature of their mission, while the second crew of oarsmen were fed at the oar and rowed in relays or took no sleep in their efforts to catch up; so they just got there in time, and only the leaders of the revolt were punished. The first decision had been hasty and wrong. Happily, there was a chance to put it right.[8]

Twenty-one years later the war was going badly for Athens. With the situation in mainland Greece locked in stalemate, they had lost vast amounts of men, money and ships in a disastrous attempt to conquer Sicily. Now their allies were revolting, the Spartans were knocking on their gates and they were down to their last fleet. They had even resorted to using slaves as rowers, not just citizens as before. Yet amazingly they won a great victory in a sea-battle near the Arginusae Islands (across the Aegean Sea, not far from the island of Lesbos) in 406 BC.

But what happened next is a frightening echo from the past. The generals who reported back to the Athenian assembly were accused of failing to pick up survivors after the battle. They replied that they had instructed some captains to do that task, but storms had made it impossible. The next day was the Apaturia, a festival when families got together, and it was painfully obvious that many were missing because of the losses in the sea-battle. The mood changed, especially when a man shouted out in the assembly that his brother was among those who had been left to drown, clinging onto a barrel and asking a mate, if he survived, to tell them back at Athens that it was the fault of the generals that the survivors had not been rescued. The cry went up that all the generals present should be

---

[8] See Thucydides III.37-50. The historian must have felt that a detailed description of this significant debate and its aftermath was needed.

put to death. Socrates, who happened to be that day's president of the assembly, refused to put this illegal motion to the vote. But the crowd got their way, and the sentence was carried out that very night. Soon there was a change of heart, and it came to light that the man shouting in the assembly was a fraud and didn't even have any brothers. But it was too late to bring the innocent generals back to life. Haste won the day; and such haste in making decisions was undoubtedly a major factor in the final defeat of Athens two years later.[9]

This chapter began with a proverb. In the Old Testament King Solomon was a great collector of proverbs and wise sayings, and he was probably the main author of the books entitled Proverbs and Ecclesiastes. Solomon lived during the 10th century BC and was famed for his wisdom. But if he had been around in 5th century BC Athens, what influence might he have had on the above events? Whether it is in the sphere of temper, or planning your life, or gaining wealth, or litigation, or conversation, or prayer, again and again he stresses that haste is the enemy of success and good sense.

- "A patient man has great understanding, but a quick-tempered man displays folly." (Proverbs 14.29)

- "Do not be quickly provoked in your spirit, for anger resides in the lap of fools." (Ecclesiastes 7.9)

- "It is not good to have zeal without knowledge, nor to be hasty and miss the way. A man's own folly ruins his life, yet his heart rages against the Lord." (Proverbs 19.2-3)

---

9 The account of the battle and the events that followed can be found in Xenophon *Hellenica* 1.6.1-1.7.35.

- "An inheritance quickly gained at the beginning will not be blessed at the end." (Proverbs 20.21)

- "The plans of the diligent lead to profit as surely as haste leads to poverty." (Proverbs 21.5)

- "What you have seen with your eyes do not bring hastily to court, for what will you do in the end if your neighbour puts you to shame?" (Proverbs 25.7-8)

- "Do you see a man who speaks in haste? There is more hope for a fool than for him." (Proverbs 29.20)

- "Do not be quick with your mouth, do not be hasty in your heart to utter anything before God. God is in heaven and you are on earth, so let your words be few." (Ecclesiastes 5.2)

Everything here harmonises with New Testament teaching. Jesus in a well-known parable talks about a farmer sowing seed. Some of it lands on a pathway, some among thorns, some on rocky ground and some of it on good soil. The seed on rocky ground grows rapidly but soon withers because it has no deep roots, whereas the seed in good soil "stands for those with a noble and good heart, who hear the word, retain it, and by persevering produce a crop" (Luke 8.15). Shallow roots and rapid initial growth produce little fruit in the long run. Haste and maturity don't often go together.

In the letter of James we find a similar lesson drawn from the work of a farmer: "Be patient, then, until the Lord's coming. See how the farmer waits for the land to yield its valuable crop and how patient he is for the autumn and spring rains. You too, be patient and stand firm, because the Lord's coming is near" (James 5.7-8).

Waiting, patience and deep roots are needed in order to be fruitful and to remain firm in the face of attack, criticism and persecution.

Saint Paul would agree. "But the fruit of the Spirit is… patience…", he writes to the Galatian church (Galatians 5.22). Similarly, when it comes to choosing leaders and commissioning them, his advice to the young leader Timothy is "Do not be hasty in the laying on of hands" (1 Timothy 5.22).

Both the Old and the New Testament speak with one voice: haste is not the pathway to spiritual growth and wise decisions.

Chapter 14

DISUNITY

~

The great war between Athens and Sparta, the Peloponnesian War (431-404 BC), rolled on for 27 long years. At times it seemed like a stalemate – which was not surprising given the nature of the two leading protagonists. Athens was a sea power, whereas Sparta relied mainly on her strong army. It was a case of the elephant fighting the whale, a war that cannot be won without the elephant learning to swim or the whale learning to march!

Peace was arranged in 421 BC, but it was an uneasy truce. After a few years two cities in Sicily which were allied to Athens appealed for help against their oppressive neighbours, particularly Syracuse. A brilliant young aristocrat called Alcibiades proposed to the Athenian assembly a way of breaking the stalemate in the war. They should use their sea power to conquer Syracuse and the whole of Sicily, and return to Greece with new resources of men, money and ship-building timber. Then they could blockade the Spartans and force them to surrender.

The assembly was divided. Some supported the aging politician Nicias, who urged caution: they were only gradually recovering from the first ten years of the war, the peace was fragile, there were enough enemies at home without sailing many miles away to fight new ones, the whole enterprise was far too risky, and they should beware of the unguarded optimism of an ambitious, self-seeking young man.

However, many sided with Alcibiades, and they grew in confidence when a proposal was made that they should go with even larger quantities of men, ships and money than the 60 ships that had been proposed originally. With such strength, what could possibly go wrong?

But they hedged their bets. They chose a trio of generals. These were the cautious but hitherto lucky Nicias, the dashing Alcibiades, and the efficient soldier Lamachus. This was a recipe for disaster; and it was made worse by a curious incident in the summer of 415 BC. One night, shortly before the expedition was due to sail, many of the little statues of Hermes that Athenians had outside their front doors were mutilated. Presumably this was the work of drunken young hooligans; but the Athenians were paranoid about tyrannical plots and started urgent investigations. The finger of suspicion pointed to Alcibiades and his friends, and some said he should be put on trial at once. Alcibiades himself was anxious to clear his name; but his opponents with greater cunning and foresight insisted that the expedition should sail to Sicily as planned while the investigations continued at home. They got their way. The ships departed from Piraeus harbour with much pomp and splendour – tempered only slightly by anxiety for the safety of their friends and relatives now that the actual day of departure had come.

In the following weeks evidence emerged that Alcibiades had been involved in ceremonies parodying the Mysteries –

the worship of Demeter and Persephone at the town of Eleusis a few miles from Athens. Even if he had had nothing to do with the mutilation of the Herms, many Athenians were deeply distrustful of him and his possibly tyrannical motives, and his opponents secured the passing of a motion in the assembly that he should be recalled and put on trial.

The generals had arrived in Sicily. There they held a conference to decide on their plan of action.

- Cautious Nicias proposed little more than talking with their Sicilian friends and then sailing around the eastern part of Sicily with a display of power that would deter Syracuse from oppressing Athens' allies.

- Alcibiades proposed that they should send ambassadors all over the island to gather allies with a view to blockading Syracuse and winning control of the whole island.

- Lamachus was even more direct, proposing an immediate attack on Syracuse; but as he was the least influential of the trio, he then withdrew his plan and supported Alcibiades.

It was shortly after this conference that the official state ship arrived from Athens to recall Alcibiades. He was arrested; but somehow on the voyage back to Athens he escaped. It is hard at this distance in time to evaluate his true motives; for he made his way to Sparta, and he gave the Spartans valuable advice about the urgency of countering Athenian plans in Sicily.

Meanwhile Nicias as the senior general began to put into practice the agreed plan of gathering support and then blockading Syracuse. But he didn't act with sufficient energy. The expedition had arrived in Sicily in the late summer, and it was difficult to achieve much in the few weeks that were left before the end of the campaigning season. Worse still, Lamachus was killed in a skirmish early in the following spring. When the Athenians did eventually start on the task of blockading Syracuse with a wall from sea to sea on its western side (and on the east it was cut off by Athenian sea power), the Syracusans had woken up to the danger and were energetically building counter-walls. The drive and urgency of their leaders (the Syracusan Hermocrates and Gylippus, who had just been sent out by Sparta) contrasted strongly with the dithering of the one remaining Athenian general. The Syracusans were even strengthening their navy, while Athenian morale was sinking and Nicias was ill with nephritis. We shall look at the final parts of this saga in the next chapter, but here it is sufficient to say that by the autumn of 413 BC the Athenian expedition and a subsequent body of reinforcements had been utterly defeated and about 40,000 men had been killed or captured. How on earth could this have happened?

Aristophanes the comic poet put his finger on the root cause. In spring 414 BC he produced his delightful comedy *Birds*. In the play two Athenians are fed up with their city and go off to join the bird kingdom. Here they urge their new-found feathered friends to build a mighty wall between the air (which is the bird kingdom) and the gods up above. This will cut off the gods from human offerings and sacrifices and starve them into surrender. The building of Cloudcuckooland is a great success. It forces the gods to send an odd trio of ambassadors to discuss peace terms – the aged Poseidon, the mighty Heracles and a strange Triballian god with a speech impediment and a trailing robe. The first audience must immediately have grasped the parallel with that trio of generals who had gone to Sicily some six months earlier. Poseidon (Nicias) proposes negotiation, Heracles (Lamachus) proposes an immediate and direct attack, and the speech and dress of the Triballian god mimic the lisp and dress style of Alcibiades. The ambassadors agree to a humiliating surrender, and the birds end up victorious.

We must not press every detail of the comedy. Aristophanes is not a traitor to his country when he humorously implies that such a trio of leaders is unlikely to succeed. Yet it is uncanny how the play has so many parallels with the Athenian expedition to Sicily. The whole plan to conquer such a distant island seems to be as ridiculous as building Cloudcuckooland. Walling off the gods is like walling off Syracuse. The ill-assorted trio of ambassadors matches the ill-assorted trio of generals and is equally unlikely to agree on a plan and bring it to a successful conclusion. And if anyone doubts that Aristophanes intended the parallel between the three ambassadors and the three generals, Poseidon in his opening speech to the birds says that they have come *autokratores*, "with full negotiating powers": this was exactly the word used in the Athenian decree appointing the generals.[10] The parallel could not be clearer; and the lesson about disunity and lack of common purpose is equally obvious.

Turning to the Bible, the failed attempt to build the Tower of Babel (in Genesis 11) furnishes us with an amusing contrast to the successful building of Cloudcuckooland in Aristophanes; and it nicely illustrates the need for unity when undertaking a big project.

In the New Testament there are not many blazing rows recorded. However, Paul and Barnabas argued strongly when they were about to set off on a second missionary journey (Acts 15.36-41). John Mark had accompanied them on their first journey through Cyprus and then left them when they sailed north to Perga in Pamphylia. Barnabas wanted to take John Mark with them again, but Paul thought he was too unreliable.

---

10   See Aristophanes *Birds* 1595 and Thucydides VI.8.2 and VI.26.1).

So sharp was their dissension that they parted company: Barnabas and John Mark sailed off to Cyprus to follow up on their previous visit, while Paul chose Silas as a new partner for travels through Syria, Cilicia and eventually Greece. This dissension must have been painful; yet good came of it. Paul was able to revisit and strengthen several churches and then plant new ones in northern and central Greece. Meanwhile John Mark is probably the young man who went on to write Mark's Gospel; and Barnabas and John Mark would undoubtedly have had an important role in building up the young churches in Cyprus.

Then there were the two ladies in the church at Philippi. We do not know why, or how strongly, they disagreed; but Paul heard of their disagreements and wrote "I plead with Euodia and I plead with Syntyche to agree with each other in the Lord" (Philippians 4.2-3). He was conscious of their help and hard work in the cause of preaching the gospel when he had first visited Philippi; and he now thinks their disunity is sufficiently serious to deserve a special, heartfelt plea in his follow-up letter.

There were also disagreements and partisanship in the church at Corinth. Paul wanted to nip all this in the bud and wrote "You are still worldly. For since there is jealousy and quarrelling among you, are you not worldly? Are you not acting like mere men? For when one says, "I follow Paul", and another, "I follow Apollos", are you not mere men? What, after all, is Apollos? And what is Paul? Only servants, through whom you came to believe..." (1 Corinthians 3.3-5). Elsewhere he likens the church to a human body: all the limbs of the body need to work together in harmony, each fulfilling its proper function (1 Corinthians 12.12-27). In just the same way jealousy, quarrelling and disunity endanger the survival and effectiveness of any group of Christians.

Unity is important in many spheres of life – in families, in school staff rooms, in sports teams, in hospitals and in other places of work. Unity has always been God's purpose for his people. Psalm 133 likens unity to precious oil, and to dew falling from heaven. "How good and pleasant it is when brothers live together in unity...For there the Lord bestows his blessing, even life for evermore." If a local church feels it is struggling and ineffective, there may be many causes; but it is important to check whether disunity has been allowed to creep in and fester, thus blocking God's blessing.

Chapter 15

CAPTIVITY
~

Sicily again. As we saw in the previous chapter, the over-ambitious Athenian plans to conquer Sicily were foundering, largely owing to the caution and lack of energy of their one remaining general Nicias. The expedition had set off from Athens in the summer of 415 BC. In the late winter of 414/413 Nicias sent a gloomy letter back to Athens saying that the enemy were growing stronger; the besiegers had now become the besieged, and he himself was ill and needed to be relieved of his command. At this point the Athenian assembly made at least two bad decisions. Firstly, they refused to replace Nicias; and secondly, they reinforced rather than recalled the whole expedition – and this turned out to be a case of "throwing good money after bad".

The Athenians sent out new ships, new forces and a new and energetic general called Demosthenes. He immediately saw that the Syracusan counter-walls which prevented the Athenians from blockading Syracuse must be captured. A night attack was arranged, and it came within millimetres of succeeding.

But the Syracusan guards on their wall just managed to hold back the attackers, who retreated in panic, losing their way in the dark and falling over the cliffs, or running into fresh troops behind them and causing utter confusion. Then the Syracusans blockaded the harbour where the enemy ships lay at anchor, and in a fierce battle the Athenians were unable to break out – a remarkable turn of events, given Athens' legendary sea-power. Morale deteriorated, slaves and hired troops began to slip away, the camp was in an unhealthy position close to some marshes, and eventually Nicias was persuaded to order a retreat by land into central Sicily. But it was a disaster. The Syracusans blocked the roads and passes and made constant attacks with light-armed troops, and after six days the whole army was compelled to surrender. The two Athenian generals were executed, and thousands of Athenian soldiers and their allies were either enslaved by Syracusan households or imprisoned in the local salt-mines where the poor food, the chill of winter nights and the lack of sanitation caused great hardship.

But some Athenian prisoners saved their lives in remarkable ways. Firstly, they earned respect and good treatment by the way they behaved. Secondly, in the days when there was less reliance on the written word and memories were better, they were able to quote passages of the Athenian dramatist Euripides by heart. The historian Plutarch reports (Life of Nicias chapter 29): *"These men soon found that their modesty and self-control stood them in good stead; some of them were quickly set free, while others who remained with their masters were treated with respect. A few were rescued because of their knowledge of Euripides, for it seems that the Sicilians were more devoted to his poetry than any of the other Greeks living outside the mother country...Many of the Athenian soldiers who returned home safely visited Euripides to thank him for their deliverance which they owed to his poetry. Some of them told him that they had been given their freedom in return for teaching their masters all they could remember of his works, while others, when they took to flight after the final battle, had been given food and water for reciting some of his lyrics."* It was, therefore, a catastrophic defeat for Athens and her allies, and a miserable period of captivity and death for many in the mines; yet there was this strange postscript of lives saved by reciting poetry while in captivity.

There are echoes of these events in Jewish history. The northern kingdom of Israel had been conquered by the Assyrians around 722 BC, and a similar fate overtook the southern kingdom of Judah in 587 BC at the hands of the Babylonians. How did the Jews react to captivity? Some took it very hard: "By the rivers of Babylon we sat and wept when we remembered Zion. There on the poplars we hung up our harps, for there our captors asked us for songs, our tormentors demanded songs of joy; they said, "Sing us one of the songs of Zion!" How can we sing the songs of the Lord while in a foreign land? If I forget you, O Jerusalem, may my right hand forget its skill." (Psalm 137.1-5). For them captivity was a miserable experience: they were totally unable to earn better treatment by the same method those Athenian captives used nearly two hundred years later.

But there were some Jews who flourished in captivity. As a young man, the prophet Daniel had been taken to Babylon with an earlier group of exiles in 605 BC. When a group of Jewish young men were chosen for education, training and royal service, he remained true to his faith and his principles: he insisted on a vegetarian diet rather than the rich royal food on offer, and he kept to his customary times of prayer to God three times a day, despite the king's decree forbidding prayer to anyone except himself (see Daniel 1.5-16 and 6.1-11). He could so easily have lost his life for these actions; but God preserved him and enabled him to rise high in the king's service.

Later the prophet Jeremiah sent a letter from Jerusalem with a message to the exiles in Babylon: "This is what the Lord Almighty, the God of Israel, says to all those I carried into exile from Jerusalem to Babylon: Build houses and settle down; plant gardens and eat what they produce. Marry and have sons and daughters; find wives for your sons and give your daughters in marriage, so that they too may have sons and daughters. Increase in number there; do not decrease. Also, seek the peace and prosperity of the city to which I have carried you into exile. Pray to the Lord for it, because if it prospers, you too will prosper.... For I know the plans I have for you, declares the Lord, plans to prosper you and not to harm you, plans to give you hope and a future." (Jeremiah 29.4-11) The message from God was, rather surprisingly, to stop grieving and to flourish where you are – even praying for the city where you are in exile.

And maybe there are lessons here for those living in locations or circumstances that might not have been their first choice. Flourish where you are, keep close to God, and leave in his hands what he will accomplish in and through you in the future. Paul endured several periods of imprisonment during his travels round the Mediterranean world; but he carried on preaching, praying and writing letters during those periods. One of these was his letter to the Christians at Philippi: he writes (Philippians 1.12-13) "Now I want you to know, brothers, that what has happened to me has really served to advance the gospel. As a result, it has become clear throughout the whole palace guard and to everyone else that I am in chains for Christ". Even in prison we are not forgotten by God; even there he has plans to use us in his service.

Chapter 16

CARELESSNESS
∽

Here is a tale of two sea-battles. Footballers sometimes talk about a game of two halves, and the same can be said about the naval battles in 406 and 405 BC that effectively brought the Peloponnesian War to an end – that long war in which Sparta had been trying to get to grips with Athens' powerful navy.

We have already looked at the battle of Arginusae in chapter 13. It was a great victory for Athens, marred by the assembly's savage punishment of the victorious generals for their failure to pick up survivors after the battle. But the Athenians failed to follow up their victory. They wasted the summer of 406 BC in vague plundering expeditions along the east coast of the Aegean Sea. Meanwhile the Spartans had appointed a much more energetic commander called Lysander. He courted the Persians, who had long been sitting on the sidelines watching the two great powers in Greece fight it out. They now decided to throw their weight behind the Spartans; and that meant Persian money to hire rowers and try to match the Athenian fleet.

Lysander knew that Athens depended on corn imported from the Black Sea area: if he could cut off that supply, he could win the war by starving Athens into submission. Therefore he took his fleet up to the north east corner of the Aegean Sea where there is a long and narrow passageway, the Hellespont, through to the Black Sea. Lysander besieged Lampsacus, a rich town on the southern coast of the Hellespont; and having captured it he was able to make it his base, with its good harbour and plentiful supplies. The Athenian fleet eventually got news of the siege of Lampsacus and set off in hot pursuit. They were too late to save the city, so they had to be content with taking up station on the northern coast, keeping a watch on the Spartan fleet from a distance of just under two miles. The place was called Aegospotami, which means "Goat's Rivers". With an open beach rather than a harbour, and with the nearest town (Sestos) about two miles down the coast, they were in a vulnerable position. There was a brilliant but wayward Athenian general, Alcibiades, living in exile nearby, and he came and warned the Athenian commanders that they should move to a more secure base; but they sneered at him and reminded him that they were in command now.

For four days the Athenians rowed out across the strait and challenged the Spartan fleet to a battle. But Lysander knew only too well how easy it would be to lose such a battle, with the Athenians being superior in numbers and better at naval tactics. He drew up a tight line of ships each day but strictly forbade them to attack. Each day the Athenians waited in vain and then withdrew, growing more and more arrogant and careless in the face of the apparent cowardice of the enemy. Lysander always sent a few scouting ships after the retreating Athenians to make sure they were disembarking and not intending to make any sudden moves. On the fifth day he was ready to put his plan into action. He kept his rowers at the oar and ordered his scouts to raise a signal as soon as the Athenian sailors had disembarked and gone off to Sestos for provisions. When the signal came, the Spartans raced across the strait and caught the enemy fleet completely unprepared. Hardly any of the Athenian triremes managed to put out to sea with their full complement of 170 rowers; the rest were only partly manned or still at anchor. The result was that a mere 12 ships escaped, while about 170 were destroyed or captured and many of their crew members were taken prisoner. Thanks to Athenian carelessness and Lysander's cunning, the Spartans secured a totally unexpected victory, destroyed Athens' last fleet and achieved a swift end to the war. One modern historian wrote "Never was a victory more complete in itself, more overwhelming in its consequences, or more thoroughly disgraceful to the defeated generals, taken collectively, than that of Aegospotami".[11]

In war "Careless talk costs lives", as the old slogan said. In sport one brief moment of carelessness can throw victory away. Take football: a goalkeeper passes the ball out too casually, the opposition forwards seize their chance and suddenly the ball is in the back of the net. The Bible frequently applies this principle to life in general: take heed – don't live carelessly.

- The writer of Psalm 119 says "How can a young man keep his way pure? By guarding it according to your word" (Psalm 119.9 RSV). Careful reading of God's word, the Bible, can train our conscience and guide us along the right path.

- The prophet Isaiah has a word for the women of the nation, warning them of impending crop failures and

---

[11] Grote: History of Greece, chapter 65. Our main ancient source is Xenophon *Hellenica* 2.1.18-28.

exile because the nation has drifted away from God: "You women who are so complacent, rise up and listen to me; you daughters who feel secure, hear what I have to say" (Isaiah 32.9). The prophet doesn't spell out exactly how their complacency manifested itself. Perhaps it was in dress, in attitude, in worldliness or in a luxurious lifestyle – something was drawing them away from God's standards.

- The prophet Daniel delivered a warning to Belshazzar the king of Babylon. While the king was feasting with a thousand nobles, drinking wine without a care in the world and showing off the treasures of gold and silver captured in Jerusalem by his predecessor, some mysterious writing appeared on the wall. Daniel was a Jewish exile in Babylon at the time, and he alone could interpret the writing: Belshazzar was about to lose his kingdom to the Medes and Persians. And why? Because he did not heed the Lord. "You praised the gods of silver and gold, of bronze, iron, wood and stone, which cannot see or hear or understand. But you did not honour the God who holds in his hand your life and all your ways" (Daniel 5.23).

- Jesus told a parable about a rich fool, who had a bumper harvest and was planning to take his ease for many years to come, heedless of the possibility that he would die that very night (Luke 12.16-21).

- Paul in one of the New Testament letters had positive and negative guidance for his readers: "Be very careful, then, how you live – not as unwise but as wise, making the most of every opportunity, because the days are evil…

Do not get drunk on wine, which leads to debauchery. Instead, be filled with the Spirit" (Ephesians 5.15-18). Christians need to avoid careless living or constantly getting drunk, and to be careful to seize all the opportunities available for good works and for passing on God's message.

- Paul also had some wise advice for young church leaders. To Titus, in charge of the church in Crete, he wrote "I want you to stress these things, so that those who have trusted in God may be careful to devote themselves to doing what is good." (Titus 3.8). To Timothy, who was leading the church in Ephesus, he wrote "Be diligent in these matters [preaching and teaching]; give yourself wholly to them, so that everyone may see your progress. Watch your life and doctrine closely. Persevere in them, because if you do, you will save both yourself and your hearers" (1 Timothy 4.15-16). As a church leader Timothy needed to take care over how he lived and what he taught. The health of a local church depends on its leaders.

Care, watchfulness, and sticking to right principles – these are important keys to success in all walks of life.

Chapter 17

DEATH

There are many moving death scenes in Classical literature. Among them is the death of Socrates in an Athenian prison in 399 BC, vividly described by his young disciple Plato.

Socrates spent his life seeking truth. His great dictum was that he knew nothing; but the difference between him and others was that he knew that he knew nothing, while others were unaware of their ignorance and muddled thinking. He had a bad habit of getting people's backs up by constantly asking questions and exposing their ignorance. "What is justice?" "Justice is helping your friends and harming your enemies", replies one bright young aristocrat. Socrates thanks him profusely, then goes on to pinpoint the young man's error. Through a series of questions, he draws out the truth that harming people is a bad thing, justice is a good thing, and therefore the definition must be wrong because it contains a contradiction (Plato *Republic* 331-336).

Socrates was satirised in a play of the comedian Aristophanes, *The Clouds*, first produced in 423 BC. His scientific and philosophical enquiries were held up for ridicule.

The great thinker is seen a few minutes into the play, hanging in a basket in mid-air. "What are you doing up there, Socrates?" asks the would-be new student at the Thinkery. "I am walking on air and philosophically examining the sun", comes the reply (Aristophanes *Clouds* 224-225). Aristophanes was a friend of Socrates, though about twenty years younger, but he was not the only comedian to attack and poke fun at the philosopher. It all contributed to a build-up of prejudice and anger against Socrates, till many could stand him no longer and he was put on trial. The charges sound ridiculous: corrupting the youth and importing foreign gods. Socrates made a speech of defence before the jury of 501, who then cast their votes. It was close; but there was a majority of about 281 to 220 in favour of condemnation. At this point in the trial both sides had to propose a suitable penalty. The chief accuser asked for the death sentence, while Socrates suggested he be given free meals at state expense for life. Unsurprisingly the jury voted for the former.

But the state ship was away on a mission – an annual religious ceremony on the island of Delos – and it was against the law to carry out a death sentence until the ship returned. Many people assumed that Socrates would escape and go and live elsewhere; yet he refused the help and the urgent appeals of his friends. His country had provided for him for all his 70 years, so why should he not now obey its final demand? Moreover he believed in the immortality of the soul, so why should he not look forward to death and whatever lay beyond?

At last came the final day, on which he was due to drink the fatal cup of hemlock. Plato writes an account in the form of a dialogue between Phaedo, who was present at the execution, and Echecrates:

"Crito hearing this nodded to the slave who was standing nearby. The slave went out, and after quite a long interval came bringing the man who was to administer the poison, carrying it ready crushed in a cup. Socrates seeing the man said "Well, my good fellow, you understand these things. What should I do?" He replied "Nothing apart from drinking it and walking around until there's a heaviness in your legs, then lie down; and in that way it will do its task." Simultaneously he held out the cup to Socrates. He took it quite cheerfully, Echecrates, not trembling or changing either his colour or his expression; but looking down at the man with his usual bull-like expression he said "What do you say about pouring a libation from this drink? Is it permitted or not?" He replied "Socrates, we prepare just as much as we think is the right amount to drink." "I see", he said. "But I suppose it is permitted and indeed essential at least to pray to the gods that our departure from here to there may be prosperous. I do indeed pray so, and may it turn out that way." As soon as he had said this, having raised the cup he drained it quite readily and calmly.

So far most of us had been fairly able to restrain our tears; however, when we saw that he was drinking it and had actually finished drinking it, we could do so no longer, but in spite of myself right there the tears came in floods. I covered my face and wept for myself – not for him, but for my own misfortune, considering the man of whose friendship I had been robbed. Crito had been unable to keep back his tears long before me and had gone out. But Apollodorus even before now hadn't stopped crying, and at this point he broke out in loud crying and anger, and he caused everyone present to break down except Socrates himself. He said "What's all this, friends! It was mostly for this reason that I sent out the women, so that they wouldn't make such a cacophony.

For I have heard that one ought to die in quietness. Keep calm and be strong." Hearing this we were ashamed and restrained our tears.

Socrates walked round, then said his legs were getting heavy and lay down on his back – that is what the man had told him to do. Meanwhile this man who had administered the poison kept a hand on him and after a time examined his feet and legs and then pressed heavily on his foot and asked if he felt anything. Socrates said no. After this he did the same to his legs; and so moving upwards he showed us that he was becoming cold and stiff. Again he touched him and said that when it got to his heart he would be gone. He was already getting cold in the area of his stomach, when he uncovered his face (for he had covered it up) and said – and this was the last thing he spoke – "Crito, we ought to sacrifice a hen to Asclepius. Pay the debt and don't forget." "It will be done", said Crito. But is there anything else you want to say?" To this question Socrates made no further reply, but after a short time he stirred, and the man uncovered his face and his eyes were fixed. Crito, seeing this, closed his mouth and eyes. That, Echecrates, was the end of our friend, a man who was, we might say, the best and wisest and most just of all the people we knew at that time." (Plato Phaedo 117-118)

The death of Socrates offers interesting parallels and contrasts with the attitudes of the early Christians. In the New Testament much is said about death. Paul wrote in Philippians chapter 1 "To me, to live is Christ and to die is gain. If I am to go on living in the body, this will mean fruitful labour for me. Yet what shall I choose? I do not know! I am torn between the two; I desire to depart and be with Christ, which is better by far; but it is more necessary for you that I remain in the body." For Paul life meant serving the Lord on earth, while death meant going to be with the Lord for eternity. This was not a choice that Paul himself needed to make: it was God who would choose the moment of his death. Any attempt to cut short his life would be wrong, because it would be throwing God's gift of life back in his face.

Later, in his last letter, Paul was very conscious that the end was approaching. In 2 Timothy chapter 4 we find the same confidence as before: "The time has come for my departure. I have fought the good fight, I have finished the race, I have kept the faith. Now there is in store for me the crown of righteousness, which the Lord, the righteous Judge, will award to me on that day – and not only to me, but also to all who have longed for his appearing."

Stephen too, the first Christian martyr, faced his trial and death with amazing confidence. He had been preaching powerfully and doing miraculous signs, till some false witnesses accused him of blasphemy and he was brought before a hostile Jewish court. Luke (in Acts 7) records Stephen's long speech of defence, where he boldly analysed the history of Israel and showed how the nation had always been deaf to God's word. They were furious, but he looked up to heaven and had a vision of the glory of God. "Look," he said, "I see heaven open and the Son of Man standing at the right hand of God". With increased fury they seized him, dragged him out and stoned him to death, as he prayed "Lord Jesus, receive my spirit" and then "Lord, do not hold this sin against them". Saul (later renamed Paul) was a witness to this event. It is probable that he is the source for the words Stephen spoke, and probable too that the whole episode had a deep effect on him and paved the way for his subsequent conversion.

Later, Christians faced several waves of persecution at the hands of the Romans, starting in 64 AD, the year of the great fire of Rome (for which the emperor Nero blamed the

Christians as convenient scapegoats). In the second century AD Polycarp was bishop of Smyrna in the Roman province of Asia, now Turkey. When he was put on trial for being a Christian, he refused to renounce his faith or burn incense to the Roman emperor, and on the day of his death he is recorded as saying "For eighty-six years I have served Him, and He has done me no wrong. So how can I blaspheme my King and Saviour? You threaten me with a fire that burns briefly and after a short time is quenched; but you do not know of the fire of everlasting punishment prepared for the wicked." As he was burned at the stake, he said "I bless you, Father, because you judged me worthy of this hour, that with the martyrs I may share Christ's cup." (Eusebius *Ecclesiastical History* 4.15)

Some years ago at a church in Shrewsbury a minister was giving a Lenten talk on "Heaven is a gift; heaven is a reward; heaven is a certainty". A few days later the minister was called to the hospital bedside of a lady who had attended that talk. As he approached the bedside, he heard her repeating over and over again "Heaven is a certainty, heaven is a certainty". Even at the eleventh hour that talk had been a revelation to her and a means of rekindling her dormant faith. She died holding on to the same truths that had motivated Paul, Stephen and Polycarp nearly two thousand years before.

Matt Redman's book *10,000 Reasons* tells the story of how the song of that name came to be written, and of some remarkable instances of the comfort and strength it has brought to people going through the valley of the shadow of death. There were the parents of a two-year-old boy named Chase who had a rare and incurable brain tumour; the couple who lost their young daughter in a horrible accident; and a group of Christians in prison in Indonesia who grew in faith despite facing a death sentence: they were still singing the song 10,000 Reasons in those very moments as they faced the firing squad.

DEATH

Some are terrified of death, or at least terrified of the process of dying. Some face it with philosophical fortitude: the 20th century philosopher Bertrand Russell wrote "I believe that when I die I shall rot, and nothing of my ego will survive", and Jean-Paul Sartre wrote "Man is a useless passion. It is meaningless that we live and it is meaningless that we die". Some, like Socrates, expect that there is something beyond death and may even be eager to discover it. But there is a sure and certain hope for the Christian, who can have utter confidence in the God who loves and forgives them and who has prepared a place of unimaginable joy for them after death.

Chapter 18

ENLIGHTENMENT

Part 1 – Philosophy

Philosophy – the word means love of wisdom. But did philosophers have all the answers in Classical times, or indeed in any period since then? Did they know the way to knowledge and enlightenment?

Some philosophers sound rather proud and supercilious. According to the Roman satirist Juvenal (writing around 115 AD) there were two Greek philosophers who were very conscious of being different from their fellow men: one (Heraclitus, around 500 BC) wept over humanity whenever he stepped out of his house, while the other (Democritus, about 460-370 BC) laughed in derision.

A similarly aloof attitude can be detected in the following passage from a Roman poet: "*How pleasant it is, when the winds are churning up the waves over a great expanse of sea, to watch someone else's great difficulties from the safety of the land –*

not because it is pleasant that anyone should be in trouble, but because it is nice to see what troubles you are free from yourself...But nothing is sweeter than to inhabit the calm and well fortified temples built on the foundations of the teaching of the wise. From there you can look down on others and see them going astray all over the place. They wander as they search for the path of life..."

So wrote Lucretius, the 1st century BC poet who brought the teachings of the Greek philosopher Epicurus to a Roman audience in his great work *De Rerum Natura* (*"About the Nature of Things"*, Book 2, lines 1-16). He paints a rather smug picture of philosophers, those thinkers who know so much more than the common herd! Were all philosophers in those days so pleased with themselves? Were they all living in ivory towers, cut off from the rest of humanity?

The attitude of Socrates (469-399 BC) was completely different. He was always ready to discuss things with his fellow Athenians and to help them towards knowledge. His teachings were passed on and developed by his pupil, the Athenian philosopher Plato (427-347 BC).

What is the difference between illusion and reality? Plato wrestles with this problem among many others in his monumental treatise *The Republic*. The work is in the form of a long dialogue between Socrates and various friends discussing what the ideal state looks like and who are best qualified to rule it. In one section Socrates wants to spotlight the general ignorance about reality in most of the population, and the importance of enlightenment and education.

Imagine a large cave, he says. A long way in some prisoners are sitting bound with chains. These bonds have held them captive since childhood and are so arranged that the prisoners can only look forwards, deeper into the cave: they cannot look back towards the daylight.

Behind the prisoners is a low wall and a large fire. There are figures walking along the top of the wall – a bit like a puppet show – and the fire projects their shadows onto the cave wall which is the only thing the prisoners can see. The prisoners watch these moving shadows with interest, listen to their talk and speculate as to who they are, what they are doing and when they will pop up next.

Then one of the prisoners is released from his bonds. He can turn round and see not just the shadows projected onto the far wall but the figures themselves, and the fire behind the figures (though it will hurt his eyes at first), and eventually the daylight outside the entrance to the cave. It is to be hoped that he will then go back to the prisoners and tell them what he has seen and so educate them about the real world. But maybe he will be unwilling to go back, having once received this enlightenment; and they for their part may utterly refuse to believe what he says, and may even attack and suppress him violently.

The conclusion? Only the philosopher is enlightened and knows the difference between illusion and reality; and therefore only the philosopher is qualified to rule the state and guide others on the path from ignorance to enlightenment.

Part 2 – Mysticism

Apart from philosophy there was another path that some Greeks and Romans thought led to enlightenment. This was Mysticism. The Athenians celebrated the Eleusinian Mysteries with an annual torch-lit procession in honour of the goddesses Demeter and Persephone. What was at the heart of this Mystery religion? What did the initiated (and of course only the initiated) see, or learn, or understand? We do not know: the secrets were well guarded and must long since have died out.

But there is a chorus of mystics in Aristophanes' comedy *Frogs* (produced in 405 BC) who seem carefree and filled with happiness. At one point they sing

> *"For it's only on us that the sun shines so bright*
> *And the light with its joy never ends –*
> *Initiates who lived a life of respect*
> *For our guests and our citizen friends."*
> *(Aristophanes Frogs 457-459)*

We have no idea *what* was involved in the process of initiation; but we do get the impression that the mystics regarded it as something special which in some way gave them a privileged position. Earlier in the play Heracles had been giving directions to the god Dionysus on how to get down to Hades safely (it's a long story – Dionysus wanted to get the dead poet Euripides back to brighten up his drama festivals!). Heracles says "*And then a sound of flutes will reach your ears, and you will see beautiful light, just like it is here, and myrtle groves and happy bands of revellers, men and women, clapping their hands…They are the folk who have been initiated*" (*Frogs* 154-158). Initiation, it seems, brought the prospect of eternal bliss in the Elysian Fields after death. And that was something so much better than the dark, silent shadows in the rest of the Underworld where it was believed most souls went when they died.

Part 3 – The Bible

The themes of enlightenment and mystery occur frequently in the New Testament. Jesus himself refers to the secret, or the mystery, of the kingdom of God. He says to his disciples "The secret [*to musterion* in Greek] of the Kingdom of God has been given to you. But to those on the outside everything is said in parables..." (Mark 4.11 – and there are parallel passages in Matthew and Luke). Parables to some people seem confusing and irrelevant; but to others who pause to delve into the meaning of the story, they bring enlightenment and understanding.

John's Gospel has a particular focus on light. "In him [the Word, Jesus] was life, and that life was the light of men. The light shines in the darkness, but the darkness has not understood it... The true light that gives light to every man was coming into the world... This is the verdict: Light has come into the world, but men loved darkness instead of light because their deeds were evil. Everyone who does evil hates the light, and will not come into the light for fear that his deeds will be exposed. But whoever lives by the truth comes into the light..." (John 1.4-9; John 3.19-21). There is a choice presented here between light and darkness. Every person has to make that choice.

A few chapters further on in his Gospel John quotes the words of Jesus, "I am the light of the world. Whoever follows me will never walk in darkness, but will have the light of life" (John 8.12). John is saying that true enlightenment is only to be found in Jesus, the baby who entered the world on the first Christmas Day and whose birthday is still celebrated with lights and candles.

Socrates would say it is merely because of ignorance that people don't embrace the light: John says it is by deliberate choice. The Eleusinian mystics would say that enlightenment is a secret known only to the initiated: Christianity is also a secret, but it is a secret that all are invited to share.

The book Revelation is also ascribed to the writer of the fourth Gospel. John implies that some things in the Christian faith are hard to understand.

- He talks of "the mystery of the seven stars…the seven stars are the angels of the seven churches…" (Revelation 1.20). We gather that each church has a guardian angel, even though the function and work of such angels is a mystery.

- A few chapters further on John must be referring to the Second Coming of Christ and the fulfilment of God's purposes for this world when he writes "In the days when the seventh angel is about to sound his trumpet, the mystery of God will be accomplished, just as he announced to his servants the prophets" (Revelation 10.7). The mystery here is God's hidden purpose for the world and mankind.

- Then he talks of the mystery of evil when he refers to "Babylon the great": this was Christian code for Rome with all its greed, luxury, immorality, violence and cruelty (Revelation 17.5). Why is there so much evil and suffering in the world? It is a mystery: one day we will understand, but not yet.

In his old age John returned to the theme of enlightenment in the letter which we now label 1 John, but which may well have been the last of the 27 New Testament books to be written. "This is the message we have heard from him and declare to you: God is light; in him there is no darkness at all. If we claim to have fellowship with him yet walk in darkness, we lie and do not live by the truth" (1 John 1.5-7). We need the enlightenment that only God can give. Without it we are in darkness.

Paul is another New Testament writer who often talks about mystery and enlightenment.

- He prays for the young converts in Ephesus, "I pray also that the eyes of your heart may be enlightened…" (Ephesians 1.18). Elsewhere he talks about those who find it hard to accept the message of the gospel: "The god of this age has blinded the minds of unbelievers…" (2 Corinthians 4.4). Paul knows that enlightenment can only come from God.

- He acknowledges that even when we have embraced the faith there will be many things that we just don't understand: the King James translation of 1 Corinthians 13.12 says "Now we see through a glass darkly". There are indeed big questions and mysteries in life, like "Why is there so much suffering and evil in the world? Can we really believe in a loving God? How can God be three and yet one?"

- Paul explains the mystery of what happens when believers die: "Listen, I tell you a mystery: We will not all sleep, but we will all be changed – in a flash, in the twinkling of an eye, at the last trumpet. For the trumpet will sound, the dead will be raised imperishable, and we will be changed" (1 Corinthians 15.51-52). The Christians at Corinth had been worried about what happens to believers at death and needed reassurance from Paul.

- He describes Jewish rejection of Jesus as a mystery (Romans 11.25).

- He also uses the word mystery when he is describing God's plan for the rescue of humanity (Ephesians 1.9; Ephesians 3.3-4). He asks his readers to pray for boldness and clarity so that he may "make known the mystery of the gospel" (Ephesians 6.19).

- Like John in Revelation, Paul also talks about the mystery of why there is so much evil and lawlessness in the world (2 Thessalonians 2.7).

- He asks his protégé Timothy to ensure that church leaders "keep hold of the deep truths [*to musterion* again] of the faith with a clear conscience" (1 Timothy 3.9).

Thus the New Testament speaks with one voice: we need the enlightenment that only God can give. Without it we are like those prisoners in the cave whose vision is so limited. Even after we have received the light and begun to follow it mysteries will remain – until that day when we no longer see through a glass darkly, but face to face.

Chapter 19

FEAR

～

"The sword of Damocles" is an expression describing some peril that hangs over us and threatens to descend at any moment. The story behind the phrase is interesting.

In the fourth century BC Damocles was an ordinary citizen at the court of the tyrant Dionysius the Second in Syracuse in Sicily. He was conversing with the ruler one day and extolling the imagined happiness of being king. Hearing this, Dionysius offered to change places with him and allow Damocles to be king for one day. Damocles excitedly accepted the offer, sat down on the king's throne and began to enjoy the luxurious feasting that he imagined was a king's daily lot in life. But then he looked up. Above him was a drawn sword, tied to the ceiling by a single hair from a horse's tail and looking as though it would fall on him at any moment. In terror he surrendered the throne, realising that the danger far outweighed the benefit. In this way Dionysius, who had made many enemies during his reign, convinced Damocles that with great power can come great danger, and a ruler can never be free from anxiety.

Cicero, the great Roman orator who devoted his closing years to philosophy, commented (in his Tusculan Disputations 5.62) "Dionysius seems to have made it quite clear, doesn't he, that there is no state of blessedness for the one over whom some terror always hangs?". The Roman poet Horace, who often advocates the simple way of life in his writings, takes up the theme (Odes III.1) "No Sicilian banquets will taste sweet, no songs of the birds or the lyre will bring sleep to the wicked man above whose neck hangs a drawn sword". Chaucer in the Canterbury Tales (The Knight's Tale) makes the same point: "Above, where seated in his tower, I saw Conquest depicted in his power, there was a sharpened sword above his head, that hung there by the thinnest simple thread." Shakespeare (in Henry IV part 2,iii.i.31) would agree: the king is unable to get to sleep and says ruefully "Uneasy lies the head that wears the crown".

Have such fears died out thanks to modern science and an age of progress? Far from it! In 1961 the US President John F. Kennedy addressed the United Nations using the following sobering words: "Today every inhabitant of this planet must contemplate the day when this planet may no longer be habitable. Every man, woman and child lives under a nuclear sword of Damocles, hanging by the slenderest of threads, capable of being cut at any moment by accident or miscalculation or by madness".[12] The so-called Cold War lasted for several decades after World War Two. As a teenager in the sixties I felt that anxiety and the tension between the American and the Soviet power blocks. More recently other concerns have come to the fore, including climate change, the rise of China, the widening gap between rich and poor in British society, drugs and knife

---

12 "Address Before the General Assembly of the United Nations". *Selected Speeches*. Columbia Point, Boston: Presidential Library and Museum.

crime. These are world problems; but fear of illness might well loom even larger in people's minds, particularly in a world affected by the Coronavirus. "Why pray when you can worry?" said one cynic – and there is certainly plenty to worry about.

The Bible has much to say about fear, worry and anxiety. The words of Jesus in the Sermon on the Mount are a good starting point (Matthew 6.25-34): "Do not worry about your life, what you will eat or drink; or about your body, what you will wear…Seek first his kingdom and his righteousness, and all these things will be given to you as well. Therefore do not worry about tomorrow, for tomorrow will worry about itself." Paul, even though he was in prison, takes up the theme (Philippians 4.4-6): "Rejoice in the Lord always. I will say it again: Rejoice…Do not be anxious about anything, but in everything, by prayer and petition, with thanksgiving, present your requests to God". Peter in his first letter gives a good reason for not being anxious, and that is God's loving care (1 Peter 5.7): "Cast all your anxiety on him because he cares for you".

It is hard to trust in the invisible God, and to take our eyes off the troubles and difficulties which are all too visible around us. But if we can hold firmly in our minds that he created us, he loves us, he wants the best for us, and he is in ultimate control over the world, the various swords of Damocles that seem to threaten us will not disappear, but they will inspire less fear.

Chapter 20

BEREAVEMENT

～

There is a bench in the grounds of Winchester College commemorating a former member of staff who had been a wonderful conversationalist. On it there is a short inscription in Ancient Greek which can be translated "We have sent the sun down with our talking". It sums up the man very aptly.

The words are taken from Callimachus, a 3rd century BC poet and the author of a short but moving poem about the loss of a friend. The poem has been beautifully translated by William Johnson Cory:

They told me, Heraclitus, they told me you were dead,
They brought me bitter news to hear and bitter tears to shed.
I wept as I remember'd how often you and I
Had tired the sun with talking and sent him down the sky.
And now that thou art lying, my dear old Carian guest,
A handful of grey ashes, long, long ago at rest,
Still are thy pleasant voices, thy nightingales awake;
For Death, he taketh all away, but them he cannot take.

Poetry is difficult to translate. You can usually get the literal meaning, you can often capture the essence and spirit of a poem, but seldom both at once. Yet Cory, while remaining remarkably close to the Greek original, has produced a work of art in its own right, a moving description of the sense of loss when someone close to us dies.

It does no good to understate the pain of bereavement. Saint Paul was well aware of it when he wrote to the group of young Christians in Thessalonica (1 Thessalonians 4.13-18) "We do not want you to be ignorant about those who fall asleep, or to grieve like the rest of men, who have no hope. We believe that Jesus died and rose again and so we believe that God will bring with Jesus those who have fallen asleep in him." He goes on to talk about what will happen at the Second Coming of the Lord: "The dead in Christ will rise first. After that we who are still alive and are left will be caught up together with them in the clouds to meet the Lord in the air. And so we will be with the Lord for ever. Therefore encourage each other with these words."

In his letters Paul is generally saying things because they need to be said, or answering questions raised in earlier correspondence. Here he is responding to the Thessalonian church's ignorance about death and what happens after death; he perceives that they are grieving just like ordinary people in the world who have no eternal hope; and he reminds them of the resurrection of Jesus which can totally transform their views on life and death. Although the precise mechanics of meeting with the Lord either at death or at the Second Coming have been the subject of much discussion and dispute, the basic truth is clear – Christians will be re-united with their loved ones as together they come into the Lord's presence for ever; and therefore they should be encouraged themselves and should share that encouragement with any who are uncertain and down-hearted.

How does it work out in practice? Does the resurrection of Jesus fill 21st century Christians with confidence and hope, or does bereavement overwhelm us and suggest that we are no different from the rest of the world who, in Paul's words, have no hope? I asked some friends and members of my local church what they thought of the poem quoted earlier and of Paul's teaching about death and bereavement.

***

Pauline writes: *"Andrew had a long, lingering death. Waiting, I felt helpless. I was comforted not only in shared conversations of our youth and age but also our shared delight in music. Comfort came too from the prayers and support from my children and church friends. Reading helped me: reading Living Light twice a day helped me to hear God speaking and soothing me.*

Looking at the Callimachus poem and St Paul's teaching about death, Callimachus was unaware his friend was dying, and this news brings sadness, bitterness, greyness. But there is comfort in recalling shared memories. The nightingales symbolise beauty, immortality and freedom: death can't rob him of his friend's spoken words. Callimachus died three centuries before our Lord, so he was unaware of what we know, that Christ is our comfort and hope. Death is a reality, whether swift or slow. We will share anguish and sadness. The nightingales speak of the beauty of the Lord and our eternal rest and freedom with Him. In conclusion, grieving continues but becomes bearable. We can suddenly be ambushed by grief, but not overwhelmed. Christ has given me hope that one day I shall be re-united with my dearest love. My overall feeling is one of peace and blessing."

***

Jeremy writes: *"Breakfast. An early morning attack on the weeds in the rockery. A rap on the kitchen window. What can Janet want? Another rap. Run into the kitchen. Janet standing at the sink holding on to the taps. Pain in her eye. Overwhelming blackness. Falling. Terrified of letting go of the taps. Grab a chair. Lower her on to it. Reach for the phone. Dial 999. Calmness at the other end. Janet beginning to fall out of the chair. Hold on while I lower her to the floor – the cold tiles which she always hated. Grab a cushion to put under her head. Back to the phone. Ambulance on its way. Open the front door – and wait. Thank God I was there and she knew I was there.*

The ambulance crew and hospital staff were brilliant. It was pretty clear that there was no hope, but the doctors kept her on life support until the evening, ostensibly while they rang round to see if anyone wanted her organs – she was a keen potential organ donor, as she had been a lifelong blood donor. But who is interested in organs from an 80-year-old not in the best of health? It also allowed most of the family to gather at the bedside to say goodbye before the life support was turned off and we saw her fade away. Thank God for the medical staff.

The next two weeks: chaos. Visits from John the vicar and Sylvia [another local minister]; choose the hymns; visit the solicitor and the funeral director; notify the bank; cards for the funeral; phone close friends; then a deluge of cards inwards. Lists, lists. Thank God for all those who helped, and especially the family who stayed in shifts.

At last the funeral – a truly joyous celebration of a wonderful life. The Church was full of old friends and new. The eulogies were upbeat, including humour, which Janet would have appreciated. Thank God for the Church, of which Janet was such a loyal and active member. Thank God for Janet.

The euphoria of the activity and the feeling that I, we, had done right by a loved friend and partner carried me through the next few days, maybe weeks. Looking back, I think there was a measure of shock, physical shock and mental shock. The euphoria, the feeling that I no longer had to worry about Janet's health, or tell her when I was going to be late for a meal, indeed the feeling that I could have a meal out, or go visiting without notice, this euphoria was soon tempered by feelings of guilt, that I hadn't always listened attentively enough to Janet's woes, that I had sometimes (often?) been too wrapped up in my own interests to give her the time that she wanted to talk, that, in her own words, I didn't appreciate her. This is bereavement: the sense that half of one's self has been taken away and the loss is irretrievable. Thank God for life.

Being a scientist I do not presume to know of the existence or nature of an afterlife. The extraordinary and unimaginable possibilities of multidimensional space-time certainly, in my cloudy view, make the existence of a Creator God, even Heaven, timeless and outside our understanding, a plausible, maybe the only plausible, the most parsimonious, though unfalsifiable, possibility. Thank God for Jesus Christ.

It is now six years since Janet died – on an infinitely distant day only the day before yesterday. One of the first things I did after Janet died was to frame my favourite photos of her from all ages in a couple of those multiple frames. I still think of her every day, but looking at the photos makes me smile. In each collection there is one photo of her smiling with me at her younger self, and happier times are recalled and I am encouraged to press on for her memory's sake.

Activity and friends soften the edges of bereavement, but the loss and loneliness are still there, though the clinical depression and self-pity are gradually lifting, with the determination to thank God every morning for another day, in which to visit friends and try to help others in what small ways I can, indeed to enjoy life. Thank God for life and good health."

***

Walter says: *"I met Meredith on a flight from Heathrow to Tel Aviv. She was an Australian nurse, and I was leading a trip to Israel. I was impressed – she was much more lively than her photo had suggested! We got engaged quickly, and we were married for nearly 10 years.*

To the surprise of us both Meredith went into a deep and long period of depression soon after the honeymoon; and a year later I got ME after glandular fever. We struggled together and so formed a deeper relationship. Hence the delay in starting a family.

There was increasing discomfort during her pregnancy, so at 35 weeks the doctor advised going into hospital to take a look. We went in one afternoon; John-Paul was born by caesarean section about 8.30 that evening; then there was an anxious 2 hour wait. Around 10.30/11.0 pm two doctors came out and said that cancer had spread widely throughout her gut; there was no hope of survival, though chemo might delay things a little. I went home about 2am, lay on the bed, and spent a sleepless night wrestling with God (like Jacob in Genesis). While I was thinking and praying, two strong images came to mind: Jesus in Gethsemane, and Abraham offering up his son Isaac. By 7.30 am there had been no voice from heaven, but I got up with two deep convictions – that Meredith would die (so I never prayed for her healing, though I was quite happy when others did), and that we were in God's hands. This certainty remained with us both throughout the last three months of her life.

Following her death, along with that underlying certainty, there was an odd, almost physical feeling of a broken heart. But the next few years were rich with the friendship and support of those who looked after J-P: a nanny during the week, and friends taking him to their homes at weekends. This gave me free Saturdays, followed by Sundays visiting those friends before taking J-P home. The feeling of being in God's hands lasted. My body seemed to shut down, and I lost 2 stone and didn't sleep well. But on the first anniversary I had a very strong sense of God's presence throughout the day; and I went for our favourite walk in Weardale.

27 years later, there is no real difference. Fundamentally faith comes down to trust – and trust is at its most real when we don't understand or like what is happening. I simply trusted, and I make no attempt to justify God's ways. We just don't know, and won't know this side of eternity: we see "through a glass darkly". We can't rationalise tragedies and disasters. I do know the Callimachus poem with its elegant simplicity. Many great poems touch on mortality, death and grief in simple and moving words, for example Tennyson's "Break, break, break" which contains these lines:

*"But O for the touch of a vanish'd hand,
And the sound of a voice that is still!".*

I suspect I am untypical in having that sense of being in God's hands. I loved Meredith utterly. It was two years till it stopped hurting and I began to recover a sense of normality. But after four years I was ready to move on. Unlike in Hollywood films, grief takes years!

***

Part 3

LATIN LITERATURE AND ROMAN HISTORY

Chapter 21

TRAINING

~

The Roman army laid great emphasis on training and discipline. In Rome's earliest years they had called up farmers and the richer citizens to form an army, and they had only done that in emergencies. But by 100 BC the soldiers were becoming much more professional. They were paid. They were better equipped. The training was rigorous. If the centurion called out the order for the tortoise formation, a wall and a roof of shields would instantly appear – and woe betide the soldier who left a small gap between the shields! Flavius Josephus, a Jewish writer, was most impressed by their training and described their exercises as bloodless battles and their battles as bloody exercises.[13] By the time of the first emperor Augustus there were 28 legions, each consisting of 5000 men, and the soldiers signed on for 25 years. New recruits needed to be strong and keen-eyed; and training would begin as soon as they joined up, probably at the age of 18.

---

[13] Josephus *The Jewish Wars* 3.70-75

But now we will turn the clock back to the third century BC, when the army had not been so professionally organised and they came up against a remarkable foe. Hannibal was born in Carthage, on the north coast of Africa. He was one of the greatest generals ever. He inspired his troops. He overcame the toughest obstacles and led them to victory after victory. He came very close to destroying Rome. And it all started in childhood.

The story goes[14] that Hamilcar, Hannibal's father, was about to lead his army across to Spain: he wanted to advance Carthaginian interests there and gain new allies before turning his attention to an attack on Rome. Hannibal was still a boy, aged about nine; but, using all the wheedling ways children have, he begged his father to let him go to Spain with the army. Hamilcar was at that very moment offering a sacrifice for the success of his mission; so he led the young lad to the altar. There he told him to place his hand on the sacrifice and swear eternal hatred towards the Romans. The boy did so; and he kept his promise.

There had been a previous war between Rome and Carthage (264-241 BC): Rome had triumphed and had won her first overseas possessions in the shape of Sicily and Sardinia. Now Carthage wanted revenge. But Hamilcar did not live long enough to start a second war. Nor did his successor, his son-in-law Hasdrubal. By this time Hannibal had reached the age of 26 and was ready to assume the command. The Romans were alarmed at continuing Carthaginian expansion in Spain and eventually declared war. Hannibal therefore set out from Spain with a large force including elephants.

It was reasonable to expect he would come by sea, as the overland route from Spain to northern Italy has various

---

[14] It is told by the Roman historian Livy (59 BC – 17 AD) in Book XXI chapter 1, though perhaps with exaggeration and embellishment.

obstacles, including the Pyrenees mountains, the river Rhone and the Alps. But Hannibal did the unexpected. He got the elephants across the Rhone by covering rafts with earth and vegetation so that they looked like pieces of land.[15] The steep and slippery slopes of the Alps presented different problems, but Hannibal overcame them and arrived in northern Italy late in 218 BC.

Over the next three years the Carthaginians won a string of victories. At one point Hannibal contracted ophthalmia in the marshes of northern Italy and lost his sight in one eye; yet this did not dampen his determination. The cavalry skirmish at the river Ticinus was a comparatively minor affair; but victory at the river Trebia was more significant, won thanks to an outflanking movement and an ambush. Then came the well-planned ambush at Lake Trasimene, where there is a valley between the mountains and the lake with a narrow pass at each end. Hannibal lured his enemy into this valley on a misty morning. The Carthaginian troops charged down the mountainside. The Romans were thrown into utter confusion; some were even driven into the lake and drowned there; and when the mist cleared 15,000 of them had been killed.

The Romans now resorted to delaying tactics: they shadowed Hannibal but avoided pitched battle. However, some of Rome's leaders were fed up with inaction, and a year later they risked battle at Cannae – a name that would send shivers down Roman spines for many years to come. Here again Rome was utterly defeated. The consul Aemilius Paulus had urged caution but could not restrain his colleague Terentius Varro. Paulus was killed along with about 50,000 out of an army of 70,000. That was the signal for Rome's allies in the south to revolt. What an amazing victory!

---

15 See the delightfully vivid account in Livy XXI 28.

But at this point Hannibal made his one decisive mistake: he failed to march on Rome immediately. If he had done so, Rome would almost certainly have fallen, and the course of European history would have been very different. One of his subordinates cried out in exasperation "You know how to win a victory, Hannibal, but you don't know how to use it!" The Carthaginians wasted the next few years in fruitless operations in the south of Italy, while Rome gradually recovered her strength. In 207 BC Hannibal's brother was bringing reinforcements but was defeated and killed in the north. This was a crushing blow, made worse when a new Roman general, Publius Cornelius Scipio, led an invasion of the Carthaginian homeland. Hannibal was forced to return to Africa, where he was defeated at the battle of Zama in 202 BC. Some years afterwards, hounded by the Romans, Hannibal fled to Syria and later took refuge with King Prusias of Bithynia, just south of the Black Sea. He still nursed plans for revenge; but when some Roman ambassadors came in pursuit of him and demanded that he be handed over, he took poison to avoid capture. He had been an amazing general; he had been a brilliant tactician; he had inspired a fierce loyalty in his troops; he had been totally absorbed in his hatred of Rome; and it had all begun when he swore that oath as a boy.

"Train a child in the way he should go, and when he is old he will not turn from it", says Proverbs 22.6. King Solomon may have been the first to enunciate this proverb, or he may have picked it up in the course of his studies. Certainly the early chapters of Proverbs are full of warnings and advice to the young.

Paul in the New Testament would have agreed with this emphasis on training the young: he was very impressed with his protégé Timothy and wrote "I have been reminded of your sincere faith, which first lived in your grandmother Lois and your mother Eunice and, I am persuaded, now lives in you also.... Continue in what you have learned and have become convinced of, because you know those from whom you learned it, and how from infancy you have known the holy Scriptures which are able to make you wise for salvation through faith in Christ Jesus" (2 Timothy 1.5 and 3.14-15). Clearly Timothy had received good training and guidance from his mother and grandmother during his youth, and with further input from Paul he became an important leader in the early years of the spread of Christianity.

Other walks of life demonstrate the same truth – that the early years can be most important and formative. Tiger Woods is among the all-time greats of golf, and there is a delightful video of him swinging a plastic golf club at the age of about 3. Maxim Vengerov started playing the violin at the age of 5, and Itzhak Perlman at the age of 3: subsequently both became superb soloists. I did once hear of a professional cellist who had only taken up the instrument at the age of 40. But such people are the exception rather than the rule, particularly with musical instruments.

Fortunately the situation is different with Christianity, and latecomers to faith are not excluded: far from it. Jesus' parable in Matthew 20.1-16 of the workers in the vineyard (who were all paid the same, however many or few hours they had worked) teaches us an important truth. Whatever the age at which a person comes to faith, they then need training and guidance in order to grow and become effective as Christians.

Chapter 22

PRIDE

~

In 75 BC Marcus Tullius Cicero was a young Roman not long out of university (or its Roman equivalent). He was starting to make his way in political offices and as an advocate in the lawcourts. His fame as Rome's greatest orator lay in the future. So did his rise to Rome's highest office of Consul, his saving of the state at a time of danger and conspiracy, his fall from grace and brief misery in exile, his vivid letters and the searching works of philosophy written in his old age. All he could see at this early stage in his career was his success as quaestor (a financial official) in western Sicily – an office that automatically brought him membership of the Senate and the promise of further steps up the political ladder. Here is an extract from one of his lawcourt speeches:

> *I'm not afraid that people would dare to describe another person's quaestorship in Sicily as more distinguished than mine...But my word, I'll say this: my thinking at the time was that back at Rome men were talking about nothing*

> *except my quaestorship. I had sent the largest amount of corn back to the city at a time of great shortage, I had been polite to the businessmen, fair to the merchants, generous to agents, abstemious with my friends. I had given everyone the impression of the greatest diligence in every duty. The Sicilians had thought up some unheard-of honours for me.*
>
> *I was leaving the province of Sicily expecting that the Roman people would voluntarily offer me everything. But during those days after my departure from the province, by chance I had taken a detour to Puteoli, at a time when lots of the most elegant folk are usually in that area. And I was almost bowled over, gentlemen, when someone asked me "On which day did you leave Rome, and is there any special news?" When I replied to him "I am coming from my province", he said "Oh yes of course, I think you must be coming from our province of Africa." At this point I was angry with him and said haughtily "No, from Sicily." Then some know-all said "What, don't you know that this man was quaestor in Syracuse [in Eastern Sicily]?" Why prolong matters? I stopped being angry and made myself one of the crowd who had come to the waters. (Cicero Pro Plancio 64-65)*

Poor Cicero! One can almost see his face and feel his deflation as he realises the humiliating truth – that no one is talking about him and he is not the most important pebble on the beach.

The Bible has much to say about humility:

- "Pride goes before destruction, a haughty spirit before a fall", says Proverbs 16.18.

- Mary was awestruck by the angel's message that she was to be the mother of Jesus, and in her song in Luke 1.46-55 she talks about humility: "My soul glorifies the Lord…for he has been mindful of the humble state of his servant… he has scattered those who are proud in their inmost thoughts…but has lifted up the humble."

- Jesus warned people not to grab the best seat at a dinner party: it's better to start off in a humble place and be invited to come up higher than to start high and be demoted when someone more important arrives; "for everyone who exalts himself will be humbled, and he who humbles himself will be exalted" (Luke 14.11).

- The apostle John in old age gave this warning (1 John 2.16): "For everything in the world – the cravings of sinful man, the lust of his eyes and the boasting of what he has and does – comes not from the Father but from the world."

Does this mean that we should never show off, never talk about ourselves, never lay claim to any special gifts, never volunteer for any task even if it seems ideally suited to our abilities? Should we always put ourselves down, always hide in the shadows, always think meanly of ourselves? No – Paul helps us to get the balance right in a passage in Romans 12.2. Here he is dealing not so much with complicated questions of doctrine but with more practical matters of behaviour and how to serve the church community. "For by the grace given to me I say to every one of you: Do not think of yourself more highly than you ought, but rather think of yourself with sober judgment, in accordance with the measure of faith God has given you." In other words, don't over-estimate yourself, but don't under-estimate yourself either. We do have gifts and talents we can use. We need to assess them rightly. We should not be put off by thinking that someone else is more gifted and therefore more important than we are. God loves us all equally, and it may often be the least spectacular gifts and the quietest people that are the most effective in his service. Paul (in 1 Corinthians 12.12-31) talked about Christians being members of a body – each having a different function, some being more extrovert or showy than others but all being vital to the whole.

At a meeting I went to recently someone made a throw-away comment about how amazingly God can use a person who is determined not to get any of the glory for themselves. And I know of at least one church that was transformed a few years ago by the prayers of one humble lady. She prayed over quite a long period that a new minister would be appointed. At last it happened; but she would have been astonished and maybe embarrassed if you had told her later how important her prayers had been. She wanted none of the glory and was always very humble. What a contrast with the pride and self-importance of the young Cicero!

Chapter 23

PLEASURE

Vides ut alta stet nive candidum Soracte...You see how Mount Soracte stands white and deep in snow... This is the opening of an ode by the 1st century BC Roman poet Horace, or Quintus Horatius Flaccus to give him his full Roman name. Horace moved in exalted circles in Rome, serving Maecenas, a friend of the emperor Augustus; yet in his poems he gives the impression of a relaxed and easy-going attitude to life.

There is a remarkable story surrounding this particular poem. Patrick Leigh Fermor was a British officer in World War 2, posted to German-occupied Crete. Amongst his daring escapades was a plot to kidnap a German general. General Kreipe was the overall commander of the German forces in Crete; but one evening as his official car was slowing up at a crossroads on the way back to his residence, British officers and Cretan resistance fighters disguised as Germans flagged the car down, overpowered the driver and drove the general off into the mountains. There followed several weeks of hiding in caves and gradually working their way across Crete to a lonely beach where he was successfully taken off to Egypt as a prisoner of the British. A few days after his capture Kreipe was admiring the morning sunlight on the snow-capped mountains of Crete, and as if talking to himself he quoted the opening lines of the Horace poem, whereupon Leigh Fermor quoted the whole of the rest of the poem in Latin; and the two men realised that even if they were on opposite sides in the war, there was a far deeper bond between them – a love of Classical literature. In translation the poem goes as follows:

> *You see how Mount Soracte stands white and deep in snow, the labouring trees can no longer hold up their burden, and the rivers with sharp peaks of ice have stopped flowing. Drive away the cold, put plenty of logs on the fire, be generous – bring out the four-year-old wine in its Sabine jar, Thaliarchus. Leave the rest to the gods. As soon as they have checked the winds fighting each other on the churning sea, neither the cypress trees nor the aged ash trees are shaken. Avoid asking what is going to happen tomorrow, and whatever days fate allots to you, call them a bonus; and don't despise the sweet pleasures of love and the dances, my boy, while you are in your prime with no morose white hair. Now, at an undisturbed hour, seek the field and the courtyard and gently murmured exchanges under cover of night; seek too that pleasing laughter which betrays the presence of the girl hiding in the inmost recess, and the token stolen from her arms or her barely resisting finger. (Horace Odes 1.9)*

If this poem is a reliable guide, Horace's philosophy of life was close to Epicureanism – "Eat, drink and be merry; don't worry too much about the future". Epicureanism was a view of life which contrasted strongly with the sterner teachings and high sense of duty of the Stoic philosophers. The Greek philosopher Epicurus (341-270 BC) founded a school in Athens which cut itself off from the affairs of the city and lived modestly and austerely. However, Epicurus had a reputation for hedonistic living (from the Greek word *hedone* meaning pleasure), and his teachings included the idea that the criterion of the good life is pleasure. This led to misunderstanding and libel, and people came to regard the two main elements of Epicureanism as enjoying the pleasures of the here and now, and not worrying about the future. There are no gods; or there are gods, but they are remote and totally unconcerned with us; so do not fear any retribution after death; for the body which has dissolved into its constituent atoms after death cannot feel any pain or punishment.

A similar emphasis on pleasure is seen in the following tomb inscription from ancient Ephesus:[16]

Baths, wine and sex corrupt our bodies.
But what really makes life? Baths, wine and sex!

Pleasure is a very important aspect of human life. However, some Christians down the ages have tried to live at the other end of the spectrum – ascetics, hermits, monks, those who appear to think that if something is pleasurable it must be sinful. Are they more in tune with the Bible?

No, the Bible has a much more positive attitude to pleasure. "Every man will sit under his own vine and under his own fig-tree", proclaims the prophet Micah. And the psalmist talks of God's rich provision for us – "He makes grass grow for the cattle, and plants for man to cultivate – bringing forth food from the earth; wine that gladdens the heart of man, oil to make his face shine, and bread that sustains his heart" (Micah 4.4;

---

16 Epitaph in Ephesus of Tiberius Claudius Secundus, a slave-trader.

Psalm 104.14-15). There is nothing wrong with alcohol, except when it is used to excess. Paul writes to his young disciple Timothy "Stop drinking only water, and use a little wine because of your stomach and your frequent illnesses"; but elsewhere he writes "Do not get drunk on wine, which leads to debauchery" (1 Timothy 5.23; Ephesians 5.18). Some people have a rule not to drink alcohol at all; but total abstinence is neither commanded nor forbidden in Scripture.

The Bible is also very positive about the delights of physical love, which are explored in the book entitled Song of Songs. This is one of the so-called "Wisdom Books" in the Old Testament and was probably written by King Solomon in his youth. In the New Testament some people look at Paul's teaching and conclude that he was against marriage. Look at 1 Corinthians 7.1, they might say: nothing could be clearer than "Now for the matters you wrote about: It is good for a man not to marry". But they fail to read the rest of the chapter, and they misinterpret verse 1 because they have stopped in the middle of a train of thought. The opening of the chapter could be paraphrased "Now for the questions you raised in your letter. Yes, to *some* extent you are right in suggesting that it is good not to marry. But that could lead to temptation and immorality, and marriage is better." Singleness can be a calling: there are Christians around today who see their singleness as giving them particular opportunities for service in God's kingdom. But in general Paul is in favour of marriage.

And what of all the other pleasures in life – music, chocolate, country walks, sport, reading, films and so on? Based on the beauty and perfection of creation as described in Genesis chapters 1-3, one could argue that there is nothing wrong with pleasure in itself. Paul was setting Timothy right in one of his letters where he says "They [the false teachers] forbid people to marry and order them to abstain from certain foods, which God created to be received with thanksgiving by those who believe and know the truth. For everything God created is good, and nothing is to be rejected if it is received with thanksgiving" (1 Timothy 4.3-5). We should underline those words "Everything God created is good". Epicureanism and its close cousin hedonism are not totally wrong. What is wrong is making pleasure into an end in itself, making pleasure into a "god" and a substitute for the One who created pleasure.

And that is where King Solomon went wrong (if he was the author of the book Ecclesiastes). He tested out pleasure and found it to be meaningless. Despite amassing houses, vineyards, gardens, parks, slaves, herds, flocks, silver, gold, singers and a harem, he was dissatisfied. This is his verdict (Ecclesiastes 2.10-11): "I denied myself nothing my eyes desired; I refused my heart no pleasure. My heart took delight in all my work, and this was the reward for all my labour. Yet when I surveyed all that my hands had done and what I had toiled to achieve, everything was meaningless, a chasing after the wind; nothing was gained under the sun." Pleasure by itself doesn't satisfy. If we make it our goal and ignore the One who created so many possibilities for pleasure, it will ultimately grow stale and disappoint us.

Chapter 24

ACHIEVEMENT
~

In the TV series Yes Minister Jim Hacker is always worrying about his image and his achievements. He rashly allows himself to be interviewed by a bright young schoolgirl who asks what he has achieved as an MP and a Minister. When he lists the Cabinet and all the other important committees on which he has been sitting, she presses the question: "Yes, but what have you actually achieved? What will you look back on with pride?" Poor Jim realises the answer to both questions is very little.

The Roman poet Horace lived through the last turbulent years of the Republic and thrived in the early years of the first emperor Augustus. He worked in a secretarial capacity for Maecenas, a close friend of the emperor, and enjoyed their patronage as he devoted his time to writing poetry. As discussed in chapter 23, he was fairly relaxed and easy-going, with a philosophy of life similar to the Epicureans – "Eat, drink and be merry, and don't worry too much about the future". But one of his poems wrestles with the question of what he has achieved, and the very first word of the ode with its three long, heavy syllables makes a bold and confident claim:

> *Exegi monumentum aere perennius...*
> *"I have raised up a monument more lasting than bronze and higher than the royal pyramids, which no biting shower, no powerless north wind, no string of innumerable years and the swift passage of time can destroy. I shall not die completely, and a great part of me will escape the goddess of funerals; rather, I shall continually be growing and fresh with posterity's praise as long as the high priest climbs Rome's Capitol with the silent Vestal Virgin...I shall be spoken of as having been the first to translate Aeolian poetry into Italian verse. Wear the pride earned by your achievements, O Melpomene, Muse of poetry, and be pleased to surround my brow with a crown of Delphic bay." (Horace Odes III.30)*

Horace's prophecy about himself was more than fulfilled. Though the Roman Empire fell several centuries after his death, and Rome's high priest stopped climbing up to the temple of Jupiter on the Capitol, Horace's poetry lived on. It is still being studied in schools and universities in the 21st century. A worthy monument indeed!

A century later another Roman writer was concerned about his literary legacy. Pliny the Younger was a lawyer and held high political offices, but he is best known to us for his letters. His most famous was a letter to the historian Tacitus describing his uncle's death during the eruption of Mount Vesuvius in 79 AD. He is very conscious of how his uncle's fame will live on forever thanks to Tacitus's history. As for Pliny the Younger's own fame and immortality, one of his early letters talks about publishing a collection of those letters he had written "*with a little more care*", and it suggests that he had had his eye on publication for some time. Another letter (which we will look at in more detail in chapter 28) extols the virtues of making time in the busy-ness of life for writing something of lasting value. Another letter talks about a statue of Corinthian bronze that he has bought. He modestly admits that he is not an expert, but he believes the statue to be a fine one; and he plans to donate it to his hometown of Comum in Northern Italy with a view to displaying it in the temple of Jupiter. So he writes to a friend there: *"You therefore, as you always do everything I ask of you, undertake this task and order a plinth to be made as soon as possible, from whatever marble you like, on which can be inscribed my name and my offices, if you think these too should be added."* Pliny is trying to be modest, but he fails to hide his desire for fame and a lasting legacy![17] However, in the end Horace was right about the lasting value of a literary legacy: Pliny's statue did not survive, but his letters did.

And what have we achieved, or what do we hope to leave as our legacy to future generations? Someone has said "If you want to leave a mark in this world you need to do at least three things: plant a tree, write a book and raise a child before you leave this earth". These goals are not within everyone's grasp. But, he continues, planting a tree shows our concern for and appreciation of the environment; writing a book passes on our wisdom to the next generation; and as regards raising a child "we want to live forever, we want to make sure that our memory and our contributions are remembered. Having a child, having someone who shares your ideas will extend your presence and your influence in this world for many more generations after you are gone."[18]

---

17   See Pliny Letters 6.16, 1.1, 1.9 and 3.6.
18   These quotes are from the Uruguayan footballer Luis Suarez in his blog in 2013, though he was surely not the first person to voice such sentiments.

The apostle Paul had a rather different ambition. His letters and the book of Acts make it clear that he never married. Despite all the advantages of his birth, education and status, he wrote in Philippians 3.7-14, "But whatever was to my profit I now consider loss for the sake of Christ. What is more, I consider everything a loss compared to the surpassing greatness of knowing Christ Jesus my Lord…I want to know Christ and the power of his resurrection and the fellowship of sharing in his sufferings, becoming like him in his death, and so, somehow, to attain to the resurrection from the dead…One thing I do: forgetting what is behind and straining towards what is ahead, I press on towards the goal to win the prize for which God has called me heavenwards in Christ Jesus." He wanted to serve his Lord, whatever the cost, and he wanted no glory for himself.

In another letter (Romans 12.1) Paul wrote "Therefore I urge you, brothers, in view of God's mercy, to offer your bodies as living sacrifices, holy and pleasing to God…" and in one of his last letters (2 Timothy 2.20-21 RSV) he sheds light on how we should serve God: "In a great house there are not only vessels of gold and silver but also of wood and earthenware, and some for noble use, some for ignoble. If anyone purifies himself from what is ignoble, then he will be a vessel for noble use, consecrated and useful to the master of the house, ready for any good work." There is a picture here of many different people in the Church performing many different functions: each member is to be useful to the Master and ready for service. Interestingly Paul doesn't say "ready for any great work", but "ready for any good work". A Christian's aim should not be personal glory and fame: their lasting legacy can be a life of quiet, faithful service. That is genuine achievement.

Chapter 25

SADNESS

~

It is natural to look for an explanation for human suffering, sorrow and sadness. Shakespeare wrote of suffering "the slings and arrows of outrageous fortune". Mr O'Reilly, the cowboy builder in the TV series Fawlty Towers, tried to comfort Basil Fawlty with the thought that however bad things are, there is always someone else in the world worse off than you (to which Basil replied with exasperation that he would love to meet that person). Others have said "Life is one d--- thing after another" or "Stuff happens". King Solomon probably wasn't the first person to recognise the mix of good and evil, of joy and sorrow all around us: he wrote "When times are good, be happy; but when times are bad, consider: God has made the one as well as the other." (Ecclesiastes 7.14).

Virgil's great epic poem *The Aeneid* recounts the story of the Trojan hero Aeneas escaping from Troy on the night when the Greeks tricked their way into the city and destroyed it. He eventually finds his way to Italy, where he plans to settle and build a new kingdom. The poem is full of insights into human life. Early in Book 1 comes the phrase

Sunt lacrimae rerum et mentem mortalia tangunt.

Literally translated this means "There are tears in events, and mortal things touch the mind". But this is poetry, and the literal translation is too clumsy. Better might be "There are tears in the affairs of mankind, and the human condition touches the heart", or maybe "Life – how often it tears the heartstrings!"

We need to examine the context of this line. Aeneas's fleet has been battered by a storm and the ships have been driven far and wide over the Mediterranean Sea. Aeneas himself has reached the safety of Carthage, a new kingdom on the north coast of Africa, not knowing what has happened to all his companions. He sets off with his friend Achates to explore the city and to seek help. As he waits for Dido the queen of Carthage to appear, he sees some carvings on the walls of the temple of Juno. In amazement he recognises scenes from the fall of Troy and some of the famous warriors who fought in that ten-year conflict.

> *"While he was waiting for the queen and perusing every detail of the great temple, while he was admiring the prosperity of the city and the work of the craftsmen rivalling each other with their skills, he saw the Trojan battles in order and the war whose fame had spread throughout the whole world – the sons of Atreus and king Priam, and Achilles who had vented his anger on them all. He stood still, and weeping he said "Achates, what place, what region of the earth is not yet full of the story of our suffering? Look – Priam! Even*

here those who merit it receive their due praise. There is sorrow in life, and mortal suffering touches the heart. Dismiss your fears; this fame of ours will somehow bring you safety."
(Virgil Aeneid 1.453-463)[19]

Many of his friends and his foes were dead. Many had met cruel and violent ends. Many had been mighty and prosperous in life, which only added to the grief of their sad deaths. It all rekindled vivid memories and deep sadness – a sadness not only for those who fell but for all the suffering that human life brings.

And yet sadness is tinged with hope. A little earlier in the book, just after escaping from the storm that had scattered his fleet, Aeneas uttered another piece of wisdom, reminding us that things may feel better in retrospect:

forsan et haec olim meminisse iuvabit.

Once again, the context is illuminating: *"Recall your courage and dismiss your sad fear; <u>perhaps even these things will be a pleasure to remember one day</u>. In the midst of various events and so many dangers we are making our way to Latium, where the fates*

---

19 The queen was Dido, who had recently escaped from Phoenicia and was founding a new empire in Carthage. The sons of Atreus were Agamemnon (commander of the Greek forces at Troy) and his brother Menelaus, whose wife Helen had been persuaded to leave Greece and elope with the Trojan prince Paris. Priam was the aged king of Troy: he came to a grisly end at the hands of Achilles' son Pyrrhus on the night Troy fell. Achilles was the greatest of the Greek warriors, till he fell in the ninth year of the war, shot in the heel by an arrow: he had vented his fury not only on Priam and the Trojans but also on his fellow Greek commanders when they slighted him over the division of the spoils of war.

indicate a settled abode for us; there it is right for the kingdom of Troy to rise again. Endure, and save yourselves for future prosperity." (Virgil Aeneid 1.202-207)

There are parallels here with Christian teaching. Paul in his letters often looked forward to life after death. He did not underestimate the sorrows we encounter in life, but he also pointed forward to the far greater joys of heaven. The following two passages illustrate his confident attitude.

> "What we suffer now is nothing compared to the glory he will reveal to us later... The creation looks forward to the day when it will join God's children in glorious freedom from death and decay... We, too, wait with eager hope for the day when God will give us our full rights as his adopted children, including the new bodies he has promised us." (Romans 8.18-23 New Living Translation).

> "We are hard pressed on every side, but not crushed; perplexed, but not in despair; persecuted, but not abandoned; struck down, but not destroyed... We know that the one who raised the Lord Jesus from the dead will also raise us with Jesus and present us with you in his presence... Therefore we do not lose heart. Though outwardly we are wasting away, yet inwardly we are being renewed day by day. For our light and momentary troubles are achieving for us an eternal glory that far outweighs them all. So we fix our eyes not on what is seen, but on what is unseen. For what is seen is temporary, but what is unseen is eternal" (2 Corinthians 4.8-18).

Here Paul gives us the ultimate and complete answer to human suffering. Some may say this is too glib an argument – "Don't worry, it will all come out right in the end!" They point to lives blighted by natural disasters, accidents and illness, or war, famine and epidemics, often caused by man's inhumanity to man. Paul does not ignore or deny the troubles and sorrows of life. But while Aeneas encouraged his companions with the thought that things may soon get better, Paul asks his readers to look further into the future, to a new age after death.

This is a new age and a kingdom which the apostle John was privileged to glimpse in the book of Revelation: "Then I saw a new heaven and a new earth, for the first heaven and the first earth had passed away, and there was no longer any sea…He will wipe every tear from their eyes. There will be no more death or mourning or crying or pain, for the old order of things has passed away." "Then the angel showed me the river of the water of life, as clear as crystal, flowing from the throne of God and of the Lamb down the middle of the great street of the city. On each side of the river stood the tree of life, bearing twelve crops of fruit, yielding its fruit every month. And the leaves of the tree are for the healing of the nations." (Revelation 21.1-4; Revelation 22.1-2)

No more tears, no more pain, no more conflicts between the different nations – it is a wonderful vision. Life may be tough, pain may be excruciating, and there may seem to be no end in prospect; but with the perspective of eternity we must dare to see these things as light and momentary.

Let an ancient prayer have the last word: "Be present, O Merciful God, and protect us through the silent hours of this night, so that we, who are wearied by the changes and chances of this fleeting world, may repose upon thy eternal changelessness".[20]

---

20 oremus.org/liturgy/ireland/compline.html

Chapter 26

CONSCIENCE

∽

Agrippina the mother of Nero was a nasty piece of work. Ambitious, cunning, ruthless, she was determined that her son would be the next emperor of Rome. To that end she had put herself in a strong position by becoming Claudius' third wife. Claudius was emperor for 13 years (41-54 AD). Despite his antiquarian interests and his love of books, he could claim the glory for having added Britain to the Roman empire in 43 AD, and for showing mercy to the conquered British general Caratacus a few years later. In his closing years he was no doubt keen that his teenage son Britannicus would succeed him. But his new stepson Nero was a year older than Britannicus, and, more importantly, he had an ambitious mother. Britannicus was poisoned by servants of Agrippina one evening at dinner; and a bit later a poisoned dish of the aged emperor's favourite mushrooms carried off Claudius. Bribing the Praetorian Guard (the soldiers stationed in Rome) ensured Nero's proclamation as emperor. Agrippina's plan had succeeded.

But that was not the limit of her ambitions. She seems to have wanted imperial power for herself, or at least to share it with her son. At first it was easy, for Nero was still a teenager, unable or unwilling to shake of the maternal yoke. Coins were issued stamped with both their heads, and Nero allowed her some of the trappings of power for the first five years. However, in 59 AD his patience snapped, and he determined to get rid of her. The Roman historian Tacitus gives us a vivid account of how he set about it (Annals XIV 3-9).

The trouble was that she was still powerful and was also on her guard against attempts to kill her. The loyalty of her household staff was incorruptible, and she had taken antidotes against poison. Then one of Nero's freedmen, Anicetus, came up with a cunning plan for a collapsible boat which would throw her into the water and drown her. In the words of Tacitus, *"Nothing is such a fertile source of accidents as the sea, he said; and if she were cut off by a shipwreck, who would be so unjust as to ascribe the actions of the wind and the waves to human wickedness? The emperor would dedicate a temple to her when she was dead, along with altars and everything else that could demonstrate his piety".*

The plan was put into effect. It was the time of year when Nero went down to Baiae, on the coast not far from Naples. He invited his mother to dinner at his villa there, treated her with every appearance of honour, affection and boyish playfulness, and lingered over the final farewells as she was escorted to the ship. Tacitus describes what happened next.

The gods provided a bright starlit night and a calm sea, as though for the express purpose of revealing the crime. The ship hadn't gone far. Two of Agrippina's household servants were accompanying her. One of these, Crepereius Gallus, was standing by the helm, while the other, Acerronia, was reclining at her feet and happily talking about the son's change of heart and the mother's recovered influence. Then at a given signal the roof of the cabin, weighed down by a mass of lead, collapsed. Crepereius was crushed and killed instantly. Agrippina and Acerronia were protected by the high sides of the couch, which happened to be strong enough to withstand the weight. Nor did the break-up of the ship follow immediately, since everyone was in confusion and most of the crew in ignorance actually hindered those in on the plot. At this point the rowers decided to put their weight on one side and so sink the ship; but in the sudden emergency their own actions were not quick and concerted, and the rest by leaning in the opposite direction allowed a gentler descent into the sea. Acerronia imprudently kept shouting that she was Agrippina and help should be given to her as the emperor's mother: she was done in with poles and oars and any other naval equipment that chance had provided. Agrippina, keeping silent and therefore less easily recognised, did receive a wound to her shoulder, but by swimming and then meeting some fishing-boats she was transported to the Lucrine Lake and carried to her villa.

It is easy to imagine what thoughts were going through her mind at this juncture, and through Nero's too when he heard that the whole attempt had been bungled, that she had survived, that she could be in no doubt who was behind the plot, and that she might appear at any moment with a band of loyal soldiers to confront him. Happily (for Nero at least) Anicetus took charge, went off to her villa with a strong force of armed men and let the sword complete the task. Nero was free of her at last.

But there is a postscript. Often after the murder Nero admitted that he was being pursued by the avenging Furies with whips and burning torches, and he tried to use magic arts to make his mother's ghost stop haunting him. A few years later Nero toured Greece. In Athens the Eleusinian Mysteries were celebrated with a festival each year in honour of the goddesses Demeter and Persephone; and there was a traditional proclamation at the start of the festival banning certain classes of people, including murderers, from attending the Mysteries and witnessing the ceremonies. Nero heard the ban – and he stayed away. He had thought he could get away with murder; but his conscience knew better and wouldn't let him off the hook. (Suetonius *Nero* 34.4)

Appropriately enough, conscience is a word derived from Latin, a combination of *cum* (meaning *with*) and *scientia* (meaning *knowledge*). It is knowledge we keep to ourselves unless we choose to share it with others. Psalm 32 talks of how good it is to have a clear conscience through admitting our faults: "Blessed is he whose transgressions are forgiven, whose sins are covered...When I kept silent, my bones wasted away through my groaning all day long...Then I acknowledged my sin to you and did not cover up my iniquity. I said, 'I will confess my transgressions to the Lord' – and you forgave the guilt of my sin." Here is a clear description of how bad it feels to have a guilty conscience, how it affects the whole body as well as the mind, and how admitting our sin to God can bring peace and relief.

This Psalm is attributed to King David. Later in life he was tempted into adultery and then murder (see 2 Samuel chapters 11-12). Yet even these heinous crimes could be forgiven, if there was genuine repentance; and Psalm 51 (so beautifully set to music in Allegri's *Miserere*) expresses David's heartfelt sorrow and repentance once the prophet Nathan had jolted his conscience about what he had done.

Paul in one of his final letters (1 Timothy chapter 1) talks about the importance of conscience: "The goal of this command is love, which comes from a pure heart and a good conscience and a sincere faith. Some have wandered away from these...". He urges his young protégé Timothy to "fight the good fight, holding on to faith and a good conscience. Some have rejected these and so have shipwrecked their faith." Faith is like the sails of a boat filled with the power of the wind; and the rudder is like our conscience, keeping the boat on course and so avoiding dangerous rocks. We may or may not be good at stifling our conscience, but we ignore it at our peril.

Chapter 27

SUPERSTITION

∼

The letters of Pliny the Younger are full of entertaining snapshots of Roman life around the end of the first century AD. Pliny lived from 61/62 till 112/113 AD. He was a lawyer, a member of the Senate and an indefatigable letter-writer. He admits that his letters were carefully written with one eye on his future fame, and the style can be a bit self-centred and pompous at times. But that's no problem when the subject matter is as entertaining as Letter 2.20 below.

One of Pliny's pet hates was Regulus, who is the subject of this letter. He too was a lawyer and senator. Pliny disliked him intensely and described him as the biggest crook on two feet. Among his other vices Regulus was a conman and legacy-hunter...

Get your coin ready and listen to a priceless story, or rather stories; for this new tale has reminded me of older ones, and it doesn't matter which one I tell first.

Verania the wife of Piso was lying gravely ill – you know, the Piso whom Galba adopted. Regulus came to her. First think of the impudence of the man! He came to visit a sick woman, when he had been a deadly enemy to her husband and most hateful to her! It's bad enough if he only came; but he even sat right next to her couch and asked her on what day and at what hour she had been born. When he heard her answers, he concentrated his expression, closed his eyes, moved his lips and did some calculations on his fingers. Dead silence. When he had kept the poor woman in suspense for ages, he said "You are at a critical juncture, but you'll come through it. In order that this can be clearer to you, I will consult a soothsayer whom I have often tested in the past". Without delay he performed a sacrifice and declared that the animal's entrails were in agreement with the message of the stars. She was gullible, as you'd expect with someone in mortal danger. She asked for her will and wrote in a legacy for Regulus. Soon she grew worse, and as she was dying she cried out that the man was wicked, treacherous and even worse than a liar, because he had sworn falsely on his son's life. Regulus often does this; and the wickedness matches the frequency, since he calls down the wrath of the gods (whom he deceives every day) on the head of his unfortunate boy.

Velleius Blaesus, that rich former consul, was suffering from his last illness, and he wanted to change his will. Regulus was hoping for something under the new will because he had recently begun to court him, so he was constantly talking to the doctors urging them to prolong the man's life by any possible means. But after the will was signed, he changed character, changed his pleas and said to those same doctors "How long are you going to torture that poor man? Why do you begrudge him an easy death, when you can't give him life?" Blaesus died, and as if he had heard everything, he left Regulus...absolutely nothing!

I suspect that legacy-hunting is not dead: some of the best detective novels revolve around this theme. But superstition too is very much alive in the modern world. Unlike the ancient Romans we no longer cut open sacrificed animals and examine their internal organs for clues to the future. But horoscopes, fortune-telling, palm-reading, tarot cards, ouija boards, seances, black cats, walking under ladders, the number 13 – there are so many strange things which people trust, or fear. Why are such beliefs so common?

Perhaps the most important factor at the root of these superstitions is insecurity. People are desperate to know about the future – to discover what lies ahead for them, what if anything exists beyond this visible world, and how they can avoid danger. And the Biblical writers offer an interesting set of answers to man's insecurity.

They do not promise a life free from troubles. "A righteous man may have many troubles, but the Lord delivers him from them all" are the words attributed to King David at a particularly difficult period in his life (Psalm 34.19). Jesus himself warned the disciples "In this world you will have trouble. But take heart! I have overcome the world" (John 16.33). And Paul suffered for a long time from "a thorn in my flesh, a messenger of Satan, to torment me. Three times I pleaded with the Lord to take it away from me" (2 Corinthians 12.7-8). We do not know what that thorn was: some have speculated that it was eye-trouble, or perhaps it was some other persistent illness or weakness. But if godly people from Biblical times suffered, we can hardly expect our lives to be any different. In Psalm 34 and in John 16 there is a positive side – not that it makes the pains any less painful, but at least we can know that God is not distant or unconcerned. And in the 2 Corinthians passage God reassured Paul "My grace is sufficient for you, for my power is made perfect in weakness".

They do not permit consulting the stars or spirits or fortune-tellers to discover the future. The Old Testament has severe warnings in several places. "When you enter the land the Lord your God is giving you, do not learn to imitate the detestable ways of the nations there. Let no-one be found among you who sacrifices his son or daughter in the fire, who practises divination or sorcery, interprets omens, engages in witchcraft, or casts spells, or who is a medium or a spiritist or who consults the dead" (Deuteronomy 18.9-11). "When men tell you to consult mediums and spiritists, who whisper and mutter, should not a people enquire of their God? Why consult the dead on behalf of the living?" (Isaiah 8.19). And King Saul, whose reign had begun so promisingly, had drifted away from obedience to God and reached the lowest point when he consulted a witch at a place called Endor. The story is told in 1 Samuel chapter 28. Saul went in disguise, knowing that he was doing wrong and that he had himself expelled mediums from the land earlier in his reign. The witch was terrified when the spirit of the prophet Samuel actually appeared; and Samuel's message for Saul was no more comforting, for he predicted that Saul would be defeated in battle and be killed the very next day, as the consequence of disobeying God and turning away from him.

In the New Testament too we find the same message. In one of his letters Paul is contrasting life in the Spirit with its opposite: "The acts of the sinful nature are obvious: sexual immorality, impurity and debauchery; idolatry *and witchcraft*; hatred, discord and jealousy..." (Galatians 5.19-20, with my italics). Elsewhere Paul deals firmly with a girl who had occult powers: "Once when we were going to the place of prayer, we were met by a slave-girl who had a spirit by which she predicted the future. She earned a great deal of money for her owners by fortune-telling. This girl followed Paul and the rest of us, shouting "These men are servants of the Most High God who are telling you the way to be saved." She kept this up for many days. Finally Paul became so troubled that he turned round and said to the spirit, "In the name of Jesus Christ I command you to come out of her!" At that moment the spirit left her" (Acts 16.16-18). The message is clear: God does not want us to know the details of future events unless he sends his prophets in specific instances; and any man-made ways of trying to discover the future are forbidden.

They do not approve of anything which is contrary to trusting in God. Paul had a very fruitful time (along with much opposition) in Ephesus. Here people showed the genuineness of their turning to God by burning some valuable scrolls connected with sorcery (Acts 19.18-19). There can be no half measures: we cannot hang on to anything which displeases God and is at odds with obeying him.

But they do recommend a whole-hearted turning to God, walking daily with him and entrusting our future to him. Jesus said to his disciples "Do not worry about your life, what you will eat or drink; or about your body, what you will wear" (Matthew 6.25). He also said "Do not let your hearts be troubled. Trust in God; trust also in me" (John 14.1). Paul has the same message: "Do not be anxious about anything, but in everything, by prayer and petition, with thanksgiving, present your requests to God. And the peace of God, which transcends all understanding, will guard your hearts and your minds in Christ Jesus" (Philippians 4.6-7). Such a trustful attitude is found in the Old Testament too. David confidently says "The Lord is my shepherd, I shall not be in want" (Psalm 23.1); and the writer of Proverbs (who was probably King Solomon) says "Trust in the Lord with all your heart and lean not on your own understanding; in all your ways acknowledge him, and he will make your paths straight" (Proverbs 3.5-6). Here are strong reasons for banishing all our fear and superstition.

Chapter 28

TRIVIALITY

~

"Prisoner at the bar, you are charged with wasting your life, filling it with trivial, meaningless, pointless, unimportant activities. How do you plead?"

"Oh, I'm not sure. No, not guilty – definitely not guilty – I think."

First, rather unusually for a court of law, we will hear from an impartial expert witness. He explains that the word trivial is derived from two Latin words, *tres* and *viae*, meaning three streets – life at the crossroads, the ordinary things we discuss with friends we meet in the village or town centre. So originally the word was neutral in meaning, though it has come to acquire a more condemnatory tone.

Now the Prosecution team will call their first witness, a Roman writer, and try to establish what he thinks about life and triviality. It is Pliny again, the lawyer, senator and letter-writer. Born in Northern Italy in 61 or 62 AD, he lived most of his adult life in Rome. Today we call him Pliny the Younger, to distinguish him from his famous uncle Pliny the Elder.

The nephew was impressed by his uncle's hard work and wide-ranging literary output. Pliny the Elder read widely, always took notes, and used to say that no book was so bad that you couldn't get at least something good out of it. This mindset enabled him to produce numerous volumes on subjects as diverse as cavalry tactics, grammar, history, biography and natural history. By contrast Pliny the Younger feels he is rather lazy, and he comes across as a somewhat self-conscious and pompous writer. In the witness box he is asked to define triviality, and he quotes from one of his own letters, in which he is trying to encourage a younger man to see what is important in life.

"It's strange how on single days in the city the account of how you spent the time either adds up or seems to add up, whereas for several days in succession it doesn't. For if you were to ask anyone "What did you do today?" he would answer "I attended a coming-of-age ceremony, I went to a betrothal or a marriage, one man asked me to come to sign a will, another asked me to speak for him in court, another called me to an assessment meeting". These things seem necessary on the day you did them, but the same things seem empty if you consider that you have been doing them every day – and much more so when you have gone off for a break."

Counsel breaks in at this point to ask why going away for a break helps one to see things more clearly. Pliny continues, *"It's then that the recollection hits you: "How many days I have wasted in such boring pursuits!" This happens to me when I am in my villa at Laurentum either reading something or writing or even having time for the exercise of the body, on which the mind depends for its support. I hear nothing which I regret hearing, I say nothing I regret saying; no one in my household annoys me with nasty remarks, I myself cast no blame on anyone – except of course on myself when I write badly; I am not worried by any hopes or fears, I am not disturbed by any rumours: I just talk with myself and my books."*

There are some whispers in the gallery at this point – "My word, that all sounds boring!" and "Is he always this pompous and opinionated". But Pliny ploughs on, *"What an upright and pure life! What leisure – sweet, honourable leisure, almost finer than any work. Ah the sea, the shore, a real and secret home of the Muses, how many thoughts and words you inspire in me! Therefore you too should abandon that noise, that empty running around and those utterly wasteful tasks as soon as you have the chance, and give yourself to study or to leisure. For as our friend Atilius said so wisely and wittily, it is better to be free from work than to be working at nothing."*[21]

At this point the Defence Counsel cross-examines Pliny. Is he right in describing all those typical events in the life of the upper class Roman as boring and trivial? Isn't public service important? What makes study and writing books so special and inherently valuable? Pliny replies that public service is indeed important, but it is your writings that will survive you.

The second Prosecution witness is the writer of Ecclesiastes in the Old Testament (who may well have been King Solomon, but his name isn't mentioned in court). He puts forward a similar view of human activity. "Utterly meaningless! Everything is meaningless". And he continues "What does man gain from all his labour at which he toils under the sun?"[22] As he gives his evidence, some heads in the courtroom seem to be nodding in agreement.

Now it is the turn of the Defence team. They call as their first witness the hymn-writer John Keble (1792-1866), and in his evidence he quotes verses from his hymn "New every morning":

"We need not bid, for cloistered cell,
Our neighbour and our work farewell,

---

21 Pliny Letters 1.9
22 Ecclesiastes 1.2-3

*Nor strive to wind ourselves too high
For sinful man beneath the sky.
The trivial round, the common task,
Would furnish all we ought to ask;
Room to deny ourselves; a road
To bring us, daily, nearer God."*

When questioned, he explains that we don't need to become a monk, cut ourselves off from the real world and strive for some ethereal greatness. The ordinary things of life are important. Each day, whether filled with memorable or unmemorable tasks, can be consciously committed to God and lived for him; each day can be a context within which to draw near to him.

Another hymn-writer now takes the stand – George Herbert (1593-1632). He too quotes from one of his own hymns and makes the same point as the previous witness:

*"Teach me, my God and King,
In all things thee to see,
And what I do in anything
To do it as for thee...
A servant with this clause
Makes drudgery divine:
Who sweeps a room, as for thy laws,
Makes that and the action fine."*

The language is old-fashioned: one or two listeners in the gallery look puzzled and whisper questions to their neighbours. But he explains that everything we do can be viewed as part of our service for God; and this realisation can transform our attitude to mundane tasks – even just sweeping a room.

In cross-examination it emerges that both these hymn-writers are following the teaching of Paul in his letters; and

George Herbert feels that when he wrote that hymn he may well have had Colossians 3.22-24 in mind. This passage of Scripture is in fact quoted by the next witness, the great apostle himself. Paul walks a bit awkwardly to the stand, and people notice the constant slight screwing up of his eyes. Not an impressive figure, people murmur; but then they detect the fire in his voice and his personality as he quotes from his own letter:

"Slaves, obey your earthly masters in everything...Whatever you do, work at it with all your heart, as working for the Lord, not for men...It is the Lord Christ you are serving."

Quite a number of slaves in the Roman Empire have become Christians, he declares – even some slaves in the Emperor's household – and here he quotes another of his letters, Philippians 4.22. Paul is telling slaves not to see their menial tasks as a hard and uninteresting slog performed for a demanding master, but as service to God. And the lesson for mankind in general, he claims, is that no task is trivial, meaningless, pointless and unimportant: if God has called us to do it, we are doing his work.

It is time for the Prosecution to sum up their case. Pliny asks a good question: what did I do today? We can reply with a list of activities – showering, dressing, breakfasting, looking after a grandchild, answering emails, making some phone calls, watching a two-hour TV programme...But what did I *achieve* today? (The word *achieve* is left hanging in the air.) Then he quotes the singer Heather Small and her challenge, "What have you done today to make you feel proud?" It's a searching question: what have I done that was of lasting importance? Very often the answer seems to be "Nothing".

The final speech of the Defence team is persuasive. We can't all be a Beethoven, a Monet or a Keats. We can't all win a Nobel Peace Prize or help discover a new vaccine. We don't all have the opportunity to plant a tree or teach a child.

Why does so much of life seem to consist of trivial and unimportant activities like dressing, cooking, housework and paying the gas bill? Answer – we need to do a rescue act on the word trivial. We need to recognize that ordinary is not the same as unimportant! All those little tasks just mentioned are very important, though unspectacular. Where would we be without them? There is a gentle ripple of laughter in court at this point, though it is cut short by Counsel's final telling observation: those who give up an afternoon to sit with a sick relative may not make tomorrow's headlines, but they are doing something no more and no less important and worthwhile than a doctor, a fireman, a mother or a member of the Cabinet.

The judge sums up briefly, stressing a few points which will need careful consideration. And then it's time for the jury to retire and consider their verdict. Has the defendant wasted his life on trivialities?

Chapter 29

SLEEP

~

Why is it sometimes so hard to get to sleep? The Roman poet Statius (about 45-96 AD) beautifully expresses this dilemma. His poetry was particularly admired by Dante and Chaucer. Born in Naples, he lived most of his life in Rome, and the following is among the most famous of his short poems.

Ad Somnum – To Sleep (Statius Sylvae 5.4)

O gentlest of the gods, o youthful sleep,
What crime is mine that I alone, poor me,
Should lack your gifts? The birds and beasts are deep
In slumber; boughs are still in every tree;
Rivers are silent and the sea's at rest.
The seventh moon now marks my pallid eyes,
The seventh sun returns at Dawn's request,
But passing with chill whip ignores my cries.
How can I cope? On crafty Argus' face
A thousand eyes could take their rest in turn,

But some youth, lingering in a maid's embrace,
Perhaps keeps you at bay. Alas, return
To me – just linger here at my command,
Or lightly touch my eyes with gentle wand.

***

There are some interesting echoes and similarities in a sonnet from the English poet John Keats (1795-1821). It makes one wonder whether Keats knew the Statius poem.

To Sleep *(John Keats)*

O soft embalmer of the still midnight!
   Shutting, with careful fingers and benign,
Our gloom-pleas'd eyes, embower'd from the light,
   Enshaded in forgetfulness divine:
O soothest Sleep! if so it please thee, close,
In midst of this thine hymn, my willing eyes,
Or wait the "Amen", ere thy poppy throws
Around my bed its lulling charities;
Then save me, or the passed day will shine
Upon my pillow, breeding many woes –
Save me from curious Conscience, that still lords
Its strength for darkness, burrowing like a mole;
Turn the key deftly in the oiled wards,
And seal the hushed Casket of my soul.

***

Both poets are wrestling with the problem of sleeplessness. Both address Sleep as a gentle deity or person with a gift to bestow. Both are looking to Sleep to close their eyes. Statius was writing towards the end of the first century AD, and there are other writers of that period who testify to the difficulty of getting a good night's sleep in ancient Rome. Martial (a writer of witty epigrams, about 40-104 AD) rails against a schoolmaster who lives nearby and whose noisy classes start very early in the morning. Juvenal (a bitter satirist, about 55-140 AD) complains about the noise of the traffic, which was the result of wheeled vehicles only being allowed into the city by night: *"Here most sick people die from insomnia…You need a lot of money to buy a good night's sleep in the city"* (Juvenal Satire 3.232-235).

Neither Statius nor Keats can suggest a remedy for insomnia. Perhaps the mellifluous language of Keats might lull the most hardened insomniac; but that would necessitate learning the poem by heart for use in the night watches!

When I was a child, I used to lie awake long after my parents had said a final "Goodnight" and then crept upstairs maybe half an hour later to close the bedroom door. But I remember reading about the England wicketkeeper of the day, Godfrey Evans: when on tour with his fellow players, he had the knack of getting to sleep within a very few minutes of arriving at a foreign hotel. So perhaps sleeplessness is a genetic problem, or a purely medical problem. In either case it would be presumptuous of me to suggest a remedy. However, if we approach the problem from a mental or spiritual point of view, we may well make more progress.

1 Sleep is a gift of God. The rhythm of night and day is part of the account of creation in Genesis chapter 1; and this remains a truth whether we see the early chapters of Genesis as literal or poetical accounts. God has also given man the Sabbath, that is, one day of rest in seven: it is a gift, and it is also a command. "Bear in mind that the Lord *has given you* the Sabbath…Remember the Sabbath day by keeping it holy. Six days you shall labour and do all your work, but the seventh day is a Sabbath to the Lord your God. On it you shall not do any work..." (Exodus 16.29; Exodus 20.8-10, with my italics). Often in the books of the Prophets the nation of Israel is rebuked for turning their backs on God, and in particular for failing to observe the Sabbath[23]. Subsequent regimes like revolutionary France and Soviet Russia have tried to alter the pattern of one day of rest in seven, but without lasting success[24].

2 God gives sleep to particular individuals on particular occasions. David was in great danger in his youth, being pursued by the deranged and murderous King Saul. Yet he was able to say "Let the light of your face shine upon us, O Lord...I will lie down and sleep in peace, for you alone, O Lord, make me dwell in safety" (Psalm 4.6-8). We can also remember the prophet Elijah after the great victory over the prophets of Baal on Mount Carmel. He was very tired and depressed; he told God in a prayer that he had had enough and wanted to die; but God's remedy was to give him sleep and then food and various new tasks (1 Kings 19.3-8).

3 Being awake is an opportunity – a moment for meditation, prayer and drawing near to God. An old hymn by Bishop Thomas Ken (1637-1711) expresses this well, though in old-fashioned language:

O may my soul on Thee repose,
And may sweet sleep mine eyelids close;
Sleep that may me more vig'rous make,

---

[23] See for example Isaiah 56.2-6, Isaiah 58.13-14, Jeremiah 17.19-27 and Amos 8.5.

[24] See en.wikipedia.org/wiki/French_Republican_calendar and en.wikipedia.org/wiki/Soviet_calendar

To serve my God when I awake.
When in the night I sleepless lie,
My soul with heavenly thoughts supply;
Let no ill dreams disturb my rest,
No power of darkness me molest.

Perhaps we can see sleeplessness as a friend, not a foe – and that might well transform the situation. But if that hymn (which is in the form of a prayer) achieves little, maybe the following story will suggest a more effective remedy:

"Towards the close of one of my nights of suffering, at half past four, I asked my kind watcher…to read me a chapter of the Word of God. He proposed the eighth of the Epistle to the Romans. I assented, but with the request that, to secure the connection of ideas, he would go back to the sixth, and even to the fifth. We read in succession the four chapters, v, vi, vii, viii, and I thought no more of sleep…Then we read the ninth, and the remaining passages, to the end, with an interest always equal and sustained; and then the first four, that nothing might be lost. About two hours had passed…I cannot tell you how I was struck, in thus reading the Epistle as a whole, with the seal of divinity, of truth, of holiness, of love, and of power, which is impressed on every page, on every word. We felt, my young friend and I…that we were listening to a voice from heaven."[25]

4 There may be underlying causes of sleeplessness – worry, or over-tiredness, or over-excitement, or not switching off properly from the duties of the day. "Natural" remedies might help, like listening to quiet music, reading a light and undemanding

---

25 A. Monod (19th century French preacher) Adieux V, Quelque Mots sur la Lecture de la Bible. The story is quoted in H.C.G. Moule The Epistle of St Paul to the Romans page xvi

book, or having a drink of hot cocoa. The NHS has some good advice (see for example www.nhs.uk/conditions/insomnia/) or various phone apps are available.

But these remedies wouldn't have helped the Persian King Darius (see Daniel chapter 6), who had been tricked by his courtiers into passing a law about prayer: it led to having to condemn his favourite and blameless minister Daniel to be thrown into the lions' den, because he still addressed prayers to his God rather than to the king. Darius spent a sleepless night, refusing food and entertainment. He had been caught in an impossible situation – and it was all his own fault. The next morning he rushed to the lions' den. There he found to his relief that the lions had left Daniel unharmed. The moral? When we are really worried about an issue and cannot get it out of our heads, the Lord knows all about it anyway, so we can act on Peter's advice to "Cast all your anxiety on him because he cares for you" (1 Peter 5.7).

5 Sleep is a reminder of our mortality. Sleep is quite often used as a metaphor for death in the Bible. Stephen, the first Christian martyr, prayed for those who were stoning him and then "fell asleep" (Acts 7.60). Jesus said of Lazarus "Our friend Lazarus has fallen asleep; but I am going there to wake him up". On this occasion the disciples did not realise that he meant that Lazarus had died (John 11.11-12).

Bishop Ken (whose hymn we looked at earlier) makes the same link between sleep and death: it is as if sleep is a rehearsal for death.

Teach me to live, that I may dread
The grave as little as my bed;
Teach me to die, that so I may
Rise glorious at the awful day.

Sleep is a reminder of our need for humility before a Creator who never grows weary. "He who watches over you will not slumber; indeed, he who watches over Israel will neither slumber nor sleep", says Psalm 121.3-4. Unlike our Creator, we need sleep. Moreover, most of us cannot strain or force or worry ourselves to sleep. But the knowledge that he is constantly watching over us and can give us his gift of sleep could make all the difference.

Chapter 30

TERROR

~

There is an extraordinary and terrifying story told about the Roman Emperor Domitian – so extraordinary and terrifying that one might be tempted to dismiss it as fiction. We find it in the pages of Dio Cassius (about 155-235 AD). He wrote a history of Rome from its origins right down to 229 AD; but some of it survives only in fragmentary form or in summaries made by a later author. He was writing many years after the event (since Domitian was emperor 81-96 AD), and he had been born in Bithynia, not in Italy. All these factors might make us cautious. Yet he did hold some of the highest offices in Rome and had access to the imperial annals; and the story fits in with what we know of the character of Domitian from other sources. Perhaps there were embellishments as the details were passed round; but I suspect the story is substantially true.

Domitian invited the leading senators and equites (Rome's second social class, who were involved in business and some government posts) to a dinner. But literally the whole room had been painted black; the tables and couches were black;

it was night, and the guests were invited into this strange room unaccompanied by their own slaves. The first thing that happened was that a gravestone was set down beside each guest, and on closer inspection each found his own name written on the gravestone, along with a small lamp such as was usually hung in tombs. Then slaves entered: these were boys, totally naked and totally covered in black paint. They performed a silent, eerie dance before taking their positions at the feet of each guest. Then food was brought in, the sort of food that was usually sacrificed to the departed spirits, black food served on black dishes. Every guest was terrified, expecting to have his throat cut at any moment. Apart from Domitian no one dared talk, which made it seem that they were already surrounded by the silence of the Underworld. The Emperor talked on subjects like death and killing. At last the dinner was over, and the guests were sent home – but not with their own slaves who had been waiting outside. They were escorted in carriages and sedan chairs by slaves they didn't know, which was utterly terrifying. They arrived home. They began to breathe again. But then there was a knock at the door: a messenger had come from the Emperor, no doubt bringing orders to commit suicide. Amazingly, slaves brought in each guest's gravestone, which was made of silver…and dishes from the dinner, all made of costly materials…and the slave-boy who had waited on him at the table, now washed and fully dressed, as a final present. What an astonishing array of gifts, after such a night of terror!

Why ever would the ruler of a powerful and well-run empire behave in this way? Perhaps we will find a clue by looking at some background details.

Domitian was the second son of Vespasian (who was the first of the three emperors from the Flavian family). They had lived through turbulent times. Vespasian had been a vigorous and successful general in the early days of the conquest of

Britain from 43 AD onwards. Then he had laid the foundations for victory in the Jewish War (66-70), though it was his elder son Titus who conducted the final year of the campaign and sacked Jerusalem in the year 70. Affairs back at Rome were in chaos after the suicide of the playboy emperor Nero in the summer of 68. There followed the so-called year of the four emperors: four army commanders from distant corners of the empire briefly held the supreme office in turn, but by the end of the year 69 Vespasian had taken control and was to hold office till his death ten years later.

Then came Titus, much loved by the Roman people. His reign only lasted two years, and during it he had to cope with two major disasters – the eruption of Mount Vesuvius in 79 (burying Pompeii, Herculaneum and other towns and villas in the Naples area) and a plague and fire in Rome in 80. But he completed the building of the Colosseum, which would be so popular with the Roman masses for many years to come. Was Domitian jealous of him – an understandable sibling rivalry fueled by the father's preference for the elder son? We do not know; but writers like the historian Tacitus and the lawyer/letter-writer Pliny refer to the period when Domitian held office as a reign of terror. And this suggests that the story of the dinner party is by no means out of character. It sounds like the product of one man's sadism, or warped sense of humour, or massive inferiority complex.

There are some examples in recent history of leaders under whom life has been dangerous – especially for political opponents who are seen as a threat. But terrifying events can happen in peace or in war; they can happen in the home or the marketplace; they can be perpetrated by lone individuals or organised groups; they can be random or targeted. Often they are aimed at specific sections of society – groups from a particular nationality, political party, religion, lifestyle or occupation. Statistically they might seem rare in peacetime; but that is small comfort to those who have actually been affected. Yes, the lightning is unlikely to strike: yes, we are unlikely to be in the wrong place at the wrong time. But forewarned is forearmed: we need a place of refuge, we need some mental armour to cope with the bolt out of the blue.

In the Bible King David went through some hair-raising experiences at various stages of his life. Surrounded by extreme dangers, he wrote many of the 150 psalms in the Bible, and Psalm 91 may well have been one of his compositions. This psalm is a song describing God's protection, and it is worth quoting extensively:

> *"He who dwells in the shelter of the Most High*
> *Will rest in the shadow of the Almighty.*
> *I will say of the Lord, "He is my refuge and my fortress,*
> *My God, in whom I trust"...*
> *You will not fear the terror of the night,*
> *Nor the arrow that flies by day,*
> *Nor the pestilence that stalks in the darkness,*
> *Nor the plague that destroys at midday...*
> *If you make the Most High your dwelling –*
> *Even the Lord, who is my refuge –*
> *Then no harm will befall you,*
> *No disaster will come near your tent.*
> *For he will command his angels concerning you*
> *To guard you in all your ways..."*

This seems to be offering a 100% gold-plated protection policy; and it is true that one hears amazing stories of God's protection from time to time. Two members of my family were on Brighton pier once while the Red Arrows were doing a display. I had gone to fetch the car when one pilot flew too low and just clipped the mast of a sailing boat. The pilot lost control, but he managed to eject, and the plane flew just over the crowd and splashed down in the water on the far side of the pier. Afterwards I thought with a wry smile of Psalm 91 with its reference to "the arrow that flies by day"! On another occasion my son aged nearly two was staying at his grandparents' house when he crawled through some netting on the landing and fell down the stairs – not just bumping from step to step but straight down to the floor about ten or twelve feet below. He landed on the bottom step, his front tooth was knocked out, but no other damage was done. I feel sure that guardian angels were hard at work that day giving the protection that Psalm 91 describes.

But Christians and non-Christians alike must face incurable illnesses, accidents, disabilities, terrorist attacks and death. In the Lord's Prayer we pray "Deliver us from evil", but sometimes that prayer is not answered as we might expect and hope. Why does God seem to protect some people and not others? If God is in control of everything that happens, why are people, including his servants, sometimes in the wrong place at the wrong time?

There are no easy answers. Ever since the Fall this has been an imperfect world: in Genesis 3 Adam and Eve disobeyed God's clear instructions, which affected their relationship with God, their blissful state in the Garden of Eden and their relationship with the world around them. Some people would regard Genesis 3 as just a myth. But others would say that even if it is to be taken poetically rather than literally, it teaches an important truth about human beings.

So we have a choice. Either we can believe that God (if he exists at all) is not all-powerful and all-knowing; that disasters come completely randomly; that it is just bad luck for those who are affected; and that there is no place in the future where all wrongs will be put right. Or we can believe that God knows everything; that he is the Sovereign Lord, whatever happens in human history; that no attacks, accidents or disasters can affect our relationship with him; and that one day there will be a new heaven and a new earth, a place where all the momentary afflictions of the present world will be eclipsed by perfect happiness. Those who "dwell in the shelter of the Most High" can have the confidence to face whatever happens in this life. They don't know what the future holds, but they do know who holds the future.

Chapter 31

ETERNITY

Hadrian achieved a sort of eternal fame thanks to the wall across the north of England that bears his name. He was the Roman emperor from 117 to 138 AD. He spent at least half his reign travelling round the provinces of the Roman empire seeing what needed to be done – and in Britannia that meant a wall 73 miles long from coast to coast to keep out the Picts who lived in Caledonia, as Scotland used to be called. As he approached death, he addressed a short poem to his soul:

Animula vagula blandula,
Hospes comesque corporis,
Quae nunc abibis in loca
Pallidula rigida nudula,
Nec ut soles dabis iocos?
O poor little, wandering little, charming little soul,
My body's guest and companion,
Where will you go now,
Pale, stiff and naked little soul,
And not making your usual jokes?

ANCIENT TRUTHS

The Romans believed that good emperors became gods after death. But it seems that Hadrian's predecessors had faced life's ultimate question in various frames of mind. Nero (emperor 54-68 AD) as he desperately tried to summon up the courage to commit suicide cried "What an artist I am, perishing here!". Vespasian (emperor 69-79 AD) made a joke of it which can be translated "Ooh, I seem to be turning into a god!". So, what did ordinary Romans believe as they prepared to cross the barrier between life and death?

Did they think of the epic poets Homer and Virgil, who wrote of a dark and dingy Underworld to which all souls went, crossing the river Styx in a boat rowed by the aged ferrymen Charon? There the ghosts flit around endlessly. Some are punished – like Tantalus, unable to satisfy his raging hunger and thirst despite the water all round him and the succulent bunches of grapes that are always just out of reach. Some are full of regrets for the afflictions they suffered in life – like Dido queen of Carthage. The Trojan hero Aeneas had been blown to her shores by a storm and had seemed to promise her marriage, but the gods sternly bade him move on to Italy where his destiny lay. In despair she committed suicide; and when Aeneas (one of the very few mortals permitted to visit the Underworld and then return to earth) met her ghost in Hades, she turned away from him in silent anger as he tried in vain to clasp her insubstantial form.

Or did they believe in reincarnation? Virgil (*Aeneid* VI.713-751) describes how Aeneas on his visit to Hades received a long explanation from his father Anchises about drinking from the river Lethe, the river of forgetfulness, after a thousand years in the Underworld, and then coming back to earth as a new person. This doctrine of metempsychosis, the transmigration of souls, was derived from Greek philosophers called the Pythagoreans – for the various branches of learning were more closely linked than they are now, and Pythagoras was not just a mathematician associated with right-angle triangles.

Or did they believe in eternal bliss? Back in the fifth century BC the Athenians had celebrated the Eleusinian Mysteries. These were associated with the goddesses Demeter and Persephone. Every year there was a torch-lit procession along the road from Athens to Eleusis, and the mystics felt they had received some special insight or knowledge. The chorus of initiates in Aristophanes' comedy *Frogs* (produced in 405 BC) sing of this special enlightenment:

"Let us travel away to the flowery fields
And the meadows with roses replete.
We will play there as usual, blessed by the Fates,
With our beautiful dances so neat.
For it's only on us that the sun shines so bright
And the light with its joy never ends –
Initiates living a life of respect
For our guests and our citizen friends." (Aristophanes Frogs 449-459)

Sophocles too (an Athenian dramatist who died in 406 BC) wrote about the Mysteries:

Thrice blest are those of mortals who have seen
These rites and then depart to Hades' halls.
For life is granted there to these alone;
To others all things there are full of woe. (Sophocles fragment 719)

There is a feeling in these passages of something special seen or learnt; something available only to those who have been initiated; something that gives hope of happiness after death.

"The solemn fast and preparation, the mystic food eaten and drunk, the moving passion-play, the extreme sanctity of the *hiera* (sacred relics) revealed, all these influences could induce in the worshipper, not indeed the sense of absolute union with the divine nature such as the Christian sacrament...but at least the feeling of intimacy and friendship with the deities... those who won their friendship by initiation in this life would by the simple logic of faith regard themselves as certain to win blessings at their hands in the next". That is the verdict of one modern writer.[26] And educated Romans would have been well aware of these beliefs: the great Roman orator and statesman Cicero turned to writing about philosophy in his old age, and he suggested that Athens had given the world nothing more excellent or more divine than the Eleusinian Mysteries.[27]

A dark, ghostly, shadowy world...a place of punishment... a place from which the soul might one day return...a place of eternal bliss for those who had lived well...No one really knew what happened after death, and people's beliefs no doubt differed as widely as they do today. How seriously should we take the rather tongue in cheek poem of Catullus on the death of his girlfriend's sparrow?

"It now travels on that dark journey
To the place whence they say no one returns.
But curses on you, evil darkness of Hades,
You who devour all beautiful things..." (Catullus poem III)

In the Old Testament some of these same images persist. Psalm 115.17-18 is typical: "It is not the dead who praise the

---

26 L.R.Farnell *The Cults of the Greek States* III p.197
27 Cicero *De Legibus* 2.14.36

Lord, those who go down to silence; it is we who extol the Lord, both now and for evermore". In Ecclesiastes the author (probably King Solomon) writes "He has also set eternity in the hearts of men" (Ecclesiastes 3.11): this enigmatic saying seems to be pointing to the inner longing of human beings for survival, for some sort of life after physical death. But expressions of confidence and certainty, like Job's "I know that my Redeemer lives…and after my skin has been destroyed, yet in my flesh I will see God" (Job 19.25-26) are very rare.

But in the New Testament we find a totally different picture. John's writings in particular have the theme of eternal life running through them:

"God so loved the world that he gave his one and only Son, that whoever believes in him shall not perish but have eternal life" (John 3.16).

"I tell you the truth, whoever hears my word and believes him who sent me has eternal life and will not be condemned; he has crossed over from death to life" (John 5.24).

"This is eternal life: that they may know you, the only true God, and Jesus Christ, whom you have sent" (John 17.3).

"And this is the testimony: God has given us eternal life, and this life is in his Son. He who has the Son has life; he who does not have the Son of God does not have life" (1 John 5.11-12)

The other New Testament writers would agree with these statements. Jesus the Son of God came to bring life, eternal life, real life, life in the fullest possible sense. We need to believe in the Son. We need to hear (and take in and act on) the words of Jesus. If we do, we shall have eternal life, which starts now and continues beyond physical death; we shall have the Son living in us; we shall have a relationship with God the Father and God the Son; we shall already have passed from death to life; we shall not be condemned at the final Judgment. And that means we shall know the answer to Hadrian's question, "Where will you go now?"

Epilogue

DIVINITY

~

Often we have seen at least some agreement between the Classical and the Biblical writers. But a fundamental difference has yet to be explored. What did they think of the nature of God, or the gods?

Jewish beliefs

For the Jews God was the Creator. He was personal, not just a vague, impersonal force. He was the God who intervened in history. The Jews looked back to Abraham, the founder of the nation, who was called by God to leave his home in the city of Ur and travel westwards towards the Promised Land. They remembered the miraculous way in which Abraham and Sarah had a child in old age. Many generations later, when the Israelites had been living in Egypt for over 400 years and ended up in slavery, God intervened. He sent Moses to rescue them. He performed miracles, which eventually persuaded Pharaoh King of Egypt to let them go. He led the nation through the Red Sea – another miracle – and guided them through the desert, making himself visible in a pillar of cloud by day and fire by night. He gave Moses the Ten Commandments. The first one reminded the Israelites that God was the one who intervened and saved them: "I am the Lord your God, who brought you out of the land of Egypt, out of the land of slavery. You shall have no other Gods before me" (Exodus 20.2-3). They often drifted away from him and sinned. But forgiveness and restoration were available to them through confession and offering a sacrifice.

Christianity and the contrast with Judaism

The fundamental difference between Judaism and Christianity was Jesus. For the Jews he was a blasphemer, claiming to be God and therefore deserving to be put to death. They turned their backs on him and continued to look out for the Messiah promised in the Old Testament. Throughout Acts, which is Luke's history of the first three decades of the church, Paul and the other disciples were constantly preaching Jesus as the Christ, the Messiah; and some Jews received this message, some violently rejected it.

Christianity grew out of Judaism. Christians looked to the same book, the Old Testament, to discover God's ways. But the founder, Jesus Christ, was the culmination and fulfilment of the Old Testament – God's final word, revealing his character in a unique way. He was God in human form, 100% God and yet 100% human.

- "In the beginning was the Word, and the Word was with God, and the Word was God…Through him all things were made…The Word became flesh and made his dwelling among us." (John 1.1-14)

- "He is the image of the invisible God, the firstborn over all creation. For by him all things were created...For God was pleased to have all his fulness dwell in him..." (Paul in Colossians 1.15-19)

- "See to it that no one takes you captive through hollow and deceptive philosophy, which depends on human tradition...For in Christ all the fulness of the Deity lives in bodily form..." (Paul in Colossians 2.8-9)

- "In the past God spoke to our forefathers through the prophets at many times and in various ways, but in these last days he has spoken to us by his Son...The Son is the radiance of God's glory and the exact representation of his being..." (Hebrews 1.1-3)

These New Testament writers – John, Paul and the author of Hebrews – all assert that Jesus is God. He was there when the world was created, and he stepped into that world as a tiny baby born in Bethlehem. God intervenes.

And why did Jesus enter the world? The four Gospel writers spend a disproportionate amount of time describing the final week of Jesus' life, and in particular the events of Good Friday and Easter Day. Jesus came to die. That was because there was a problem, the problem of human sinfulness. Both Old and New Testaments make it clear that we are cut off from God, we have rebelled against him, we deserve punishment, and we cannot save ourselves. So how can this problem be solved?

- For Matthew, Jesus was the one at whose death "the curtain of the temple was torn in two from top to bottom" – a dramatic way of stating that we can now enter the most holy place in the temple; we can come into God's very presence.

- For Mark, "The Son of Man did not come to be served, but to serve, and to give his life as a ransom for many." We were captives, or slaves; and Jesus has paid the price to set us free.

- For Luke, Jesus on the cross was the one who could say to the dying but penitent thief "I tell you the truth, today you will be with me in paradise." Jesus has opened the way to eternal life in heaven.

- And for John, Jesus is "the Lamb of God, who takes away the sin of the world". Jesus is the fulfilment of all those Old Testament sacrifices that were offered to take away sin. Through him, we can be forgiven. Jesus' final great cry from the cross was *tetelestai*, the Greek word for "It has been accomplished". But it was also the word written on bills and can mean "Paid!" (See Matthew 27.51; Mark 10.45; Luke23.43; John 1.29)

All four writers move on to describe the triumphant resurrection of Jesus on the third day. This sets the seal on all that Jesus did and taught during his three years of public ministry: Jesus and the resurrection are the cornerstones of the Christian faith.

Greek beliefs

For many Greeks Homer's two great poems, the Iliad and the Odyssey, were a sort of Bible. The poems described the Trojan War and its aftermath, and the gods were deeply involved in those events. They were the immortals, the Olympians, living on Mount Olympus in Northern Greece (or some heavenly copy of Mount Olympus). They were to some extent anthropomorphic, gods in human form apart from being immortal and more powerful than men.

They had their squabbles, as we see in the delightful story of Hephaestus (the god of metal-working) and his wife Aphrodite (the goddess of love). Ares (the god of war) was having an affair with Aphrodite. But Hephaestus used his blacksmith skills to arrange a trap and catch them in the act, and he then invited all the other gods and goddesses to come along and enjoy their embarrassment. The gods had their weaknesses, for example Zeus with his frequent affairs with mortal women. They also had their human favourites – notably Athene who watched over Odysseus on his perilous adventures returning home from Troy. Her protection was important, as Poseidon the god of the sea hated Odysseus and wanted to make his journey as difficult as possible.

In the Classical period (roughly the fifth and fourth centuries BC), fine temples were built, like the Parthenon in Athens. Sculptors made beautiful statues of the gods and goddesses; and the statue of Zeus at Olympia was one of the so-called Seven Wonders of the World. Annual festivals and ceremonies were held: at Athens, for example, there was the Panathenaea (a procession up to Athene's temple on the Acropolis), the drama festivals in honour of Dionysus, and the Eleusinian Mysteries with a torchlit procession in honour of the goddesses Demeter and Persephone.

But we do not know much about people's personal beliefs, and whether their beliefs affected their daily lives. Thucydides, the historian of the Peloponnesian War, writes an epitaph on the Athenian general Nicias (who had been captured and put to death in Sicily) saying that Nicias least deserved to come to such an unfortunate end, in view of his virtuous life (Thucydides VII.86). A few chapters earlier Nicias had been very affected by the eclipse of the moon at a key moment in the Sicilian campaign: he took the view that nothing should be done for thrice nine days – with disastrous effects on the morale and safety of the army (Thucydides VII.50). Socrates was not only a great thinker and debater, but he also claimed to have some sort of divine sign which guided or restrained him from time to time (Plato *Apology of Socrates* 40). Such insights into what individuals personally believed are rare.

Christianity and the clash with the Greeks

Christian beliefs about the nature of God are very different from Greek beliefs:

- For Christians God is one – monotheism, not polytheism.

- God is moral, and he is the source of morality.

- Christians do not make or worship statues of God.

Paul was on the second of his three missionary journeys round the Mediterranean world when he arrived in Athens, as recorded in Acts chapter 17. By the first century AD the city had long since ceased to be an imperial power. But it was a city full of philosophers and a good place for study. Paul had frequent debates with people in the synagogue and the marketplace. Some Epicurean and Stoic philosophers argued with him, and he was invited to explain his beliefs to the Areopagus (an ancient lawcourt). Luke gives a summary of his speech. Paul had noticed an altar with an inscription "To an unknown god", and he told them about Jesus and the resurrection. He talked of God as the Creator, the Giver of life, the One who will one day judge the world. Some of the listeners mocked, especially when they heard the claim about rising from the dead: they misunderstood the word *anastasis* (a Greek word meaning *resurrection*) and thought this was some new goddess! But a few did respond and became believers. This story illustrates how very different Christianity and Greek beliefs were, and how hard it was for Greeks to overhaul their beliefs and traditions so radically.

Roman beliefs

Religion was at the heart of Roman life. The founders of Rome, Romulus and Remus, were believed to be children of the god Mars. The temple of Jupiter on the Capitoline Hill was a prominent landmark, and there were other temples dedicated to various gods in the forum below the Capitol. They worshipped the twelve Olympian gods and goddesses – similar to the Greek gods, though with different names. Jupiter was the equivalent of Zeus, Neptune of Poseidon and so on. There were also gods of the hearth and the store cupboard, the Lares and the Penates, as these were such important parts of the home. There were numerous local gods and festivals associated with different places and different areas of life. The Carmentalia on January 11th in honour of Carmentis (an old Italic goddess of childbirth) and the Robigalia on April 25th (to stop Robigus the god of rust attacking the corn) were just two of many.

But outward ceremony was more important than inner belief. The priesthood was more like a political office than a matter of faith and a special calling. The historian Tacitus was quite cynical about the gods: he saw them as being more concerned with punishing humans than caring for them. And yet he held a priesthood. The main aim was to keep the gods on your side, to preserve the *pax deorum* ("the peace of the gods"), not to offend them in any way.

How could this peace or favour of the gods be obtained? By sacrifices, by prayers, by fulfilling public and private vows, by purifying the land or the city (in a ceremony called *lustratio*), and by paying careful attention to omens. The job of an *augur* was to watch the flight of birds, while the job of a *haruspex* was to examine the entrails of sacrificed animals. We may well look on these strange methods of trying to predict the future with amazement or horror. But the more cautious Romans would have pointed to a former consul called Claudius. In 249 BC, just before the sea-battle of Drepana, he took the omens by testing how eagerly the sacred chickens gobbled up their food: they refused to eat, so he threw them overboard crying "If they won't eat, let them drink!" and he promptly lost the battle.[28]

With the same concern, the Romans were careful not to offend the gods of any land they conquered. Their aim was syncretism – the blending together of their own gods and the local gods. So at Bath in the south west of the new province of Britannia we find an altar to Sulis Minerva – Sulis being the local Celtic goddess and Minerva being regarded as the Roman equivalent.

Provincial governors would pray and offer vows for the safety of the emperor. A vow was a sort of contract with the gods and might take the following form: "If you preserve the life and health of the emperor over the coming year, I will pay you a sacrifice of…". In some eastern provinces of the empire Roman emperors were regarded as gods even during their lifetime; but this was not the case in the western parts of the empire, though good emperors were deified by a decree of the Roman Senate after their death.

---

[28] Cicero relates this story in *De Natura Deorum* ("About the nature of the gods") 2.7.

Of course, not all Romans held precisely the same set of beliefs. As in 21st century Britain, there were plenty of people who followed very different creeds, or none at all. The Epicureans believed that the gods did exist – they must exist, because we dream about them. But they were far off and had no effect on human life: as the Roman poet Lucretius said, "That which cannot be touched cannot touch and affect us".[29] Then there were the philosophers and the cynics – like Segius in a tongue-in-cheek epigram by Martial: "Segius says that there are no gods and the sky is empty; and he can prove it, because he sees he has become prosperous in spite of denying these things!"[30] A much later historian sums it up well: "The various modes of worship which prevailed in the Roman world were all considered by the people as equally true; by the philosopher as equally false; and by the magistrate as equally useful."[31]

The Romans tolerated the Jews. Judaism was a *religio licita* ("a permitted religion"), respected because of its antiquity. But the Christians were different, and dangerous, so in times of disaster they blamed the Christians. When fire destroyed a lot of Rome in 64 AD, Nero made the Christians into convenient scapegoats. Nearly fifty years later, in 111 AD, Pliny the Younger went to govern the provinces of Bithynia and Pontus (just south of the Black Sea). He had to consult the emperor Trajan about how to conduct the trials of Christians (Pliny Letters X.96). What exactly was their crime? Was it simply

---

29 Lucretius (about 94-55 BC) *De Rerum Natura* ("About the nature of things") 5.152: in this long poem Lucretius was seeking to explain Epicurean beliefs to a Roman audience.

30 Martial (about 40-104 AD) *Epigrams* 4.21: Martial wrote short, witty poems about individuals and society in Rome.

31 Edward Gibbon (1737-1794) *The History of the Decline and Fall of the Roman Empire*, Vol. 1, chapter 2.

being Christian? Was it crimes associated with Christians? Was it their stubbornness in refusing to renounce their beliefs? Despite threats of punishment, they were refusing to deny Christ, to call on the Roman gods and to offer incense to the emperor's statue.

Christianity and Roman persecution

There were several reasons why the Romans persecuted Christians. They attacked them because...

- The Christians angered the gods: they disturbed the *pax deorum*. Tertullian was a Christian writer in the third century AD, and he summed it up in his *Apologeticus* 40.2 by saying that when the Tiber [the river in Rome] overflows, or the Nile doesn't overflow, the cry goes up *Christianos ad leonem* – "Throw the Christians to the lion!" (To this he wittily replied *Omnes ad unum*? – "All the Christians, to just one lion?") Floods in Rome were a disaster. Lack of flooding in Egypt was also a disaster, as Egypt depended on the Nile's annual flooding to irrigate the crops, and Rome depended on Egypt for a significant part of its corn supply. These natural disasters showed that the gods were angry. Christians refused to worship the Roman gods: therefore they were to blame.

- They were exclusive: they refused to worship the Roman gods and the emperor <u>as well as</u> their own God. They claimed that there was only one God, and all others were false gods. To the Romans with their syncretistic approach such exclusivity was incomprehensible. This explains the attitude of Paternus, the governor of Africa, when Cyprian was on trial in 257 AD for his Christian faith. Paternus read out the following imperial decree: "Those who don't observe the Roman religion ought to recognise Roman ceremonies".

- They caused riots and political trouble. One of the reasons why Pilate ordered the crucifixion of Jesus was because he saw a riot brewing; and Paul's preaching stirred up a lot of trouble in numerous places, as Luke records throughout his book Acts.[32]

- They were hated for their supposed crimes. "Eating the body of Christ" sounded suspiciously like cannibalism; and "loving your brothers and sisters" sounded like incest.

- Christianity was morally demanding. Felix, a Roman governor of the province of Judaea, provides a good example of this (see Acts 24. 22-26). He was married to a Jewess, so he probably knew quite a bit about Judaism and Christianity. Paul had been arrested and brought before the governor, who was quite happy to discuss Christian beliefs with him. But when Paul started to talk about righteousness, self-control and the coming Day of Judgment, Felix hastily put an end to the discussion.

- Christianity was "a deadly superstition". So Tacitus describes it when talking about the fire at Rome in 64 AD and its aftermath (Tacitus Annals XV.44). He notes that the founder Christus had been put to death under Pontius Pilate in the reign of Tiberius. "Temporarily

---

32 See for example Acts 16.19-40; 17.5-9; 17.13-14; 18.12-17;19.23-41; 21.27-40; 22.22-29.

repressed, the deadly superstition was breaking out again, not only throughout Judaea, the source of that evil, but even in the City [Rome]". Admittedly Tacitus was cynical about the gods, omens and so on. But he was a senator and held high offices in Rome, and it is likely that many Romans shared his hostile views on Christianity.

For all these reasons Christians were hated and persecuted, and the Colosseum in Rome is one of many buildings in the Roman Empire where Christians faced martyrdom. It wasn't till the fourth century AD that the tide turned, the Emperor Constantine embraced the Christian faith, and it soon became the official religion of the Roman Empire.

At the trial of Jesus Pilate asked, maybe cynically, "What is truth?" It is a good question: in fact, it is the vital question. "Jews demand miraculous signs and Greeks look for wisdom, but we preach Christ crucified" was Paul's message to the group of Christians at Corinth (1 Corinthians 1.22-23). The Jews, the Greeks and the Romans found this message hard to accept. In Christianity the vital difference is found in Jesus Christ – the God who intervened, who lived among us in person, who weeps with us in our suffering and pain, and who even now invites us to share in his victory over death.

Appendix 1

INDEX OF GREEK AND ROMAN WRITERS

Index of Greek and Roman Writers

Numbers in square brackets give the chapters in which the writer is mentioned or quoted.

Ep = Epilogue. Some dates are uncertain or approximate and are marked c. (circa = about).

Aristophanes: c.450-388 BC, Athenian comic dramatist; 11 of his comedies survive. [14,17,18,31]

Callimachus: 3rd century BC Greek poet. [20]

Catullus: Roman love poet, c.84-54 BC. [31]

Cicero: Roman orator and statesman, 106-43 BC. [19,22, Ep]

Dio Cassius: 2nd/3rd century AD Roman Senator and historian, wrote in Greek a history of Rome from its origins to 229 AD. [30]

Euripides: c.484-406 BC, Athenian playwright; wrote about 92 tragedies of which only about 18 survive. [4,5,15]

Hadrian: Born in 76 AD, Roman emperor 117-138 AD. [31]

Herodotus: 5th century BC Greek historian, called "The Father of History", described the wars between Greece and Persia (490-479 BC). [10,11,12]

Homer: Greek epic poet, wrote *The Iliad* and *The Odyssey*, our earliest surviving European literature; he lived probably c.750 BC. [31, Ep]

Horace: Roman lyric poet and satirist, 65-8 BC. [9,19,23,24]

Josephus: A Jew writing for a Roman audience, born c.37 AD. [21]

Juvenal: 1st/2nd century AD Roman satirist. [Prologue, 9,29]

Livy: Roman historian, c.59 BC – 17 AD, composed a history of Rome in 142 volumes, only some of which survive. [21]

Lucretius: c.94-55 BC, Roman poet and philosopher who described Epicurean philosophy for a Roman audience in his *De Rerum Natura* ("About the Nature of Things"). [18, Ep]

Martial: c.40-104 AD, Roman writer of short, witty epigrams. [29, Ep]

Ovid: 43 BC – 17 AD, prolific Roman poet, exiled during the reign of the Emperor Augustus. [2]

Plato: c.429-347 BC, Greek philosopher and pupil of Socrates. [17,18, Ep]

Pliny the Younger: Roman lawyer and letter-writer, 61/62-112/113 AD. [24,27,28,30, Ep]

Plutarch: c.50-120 AD, Greek historian, wrote parallel lives – biographies comparing pairs of famous Greeks and Romans. [15]

Sophocles: c.496-406 BC, Athenian playwright; only 7 of his plays survive. [7,8]

Statius: c.45-96 AD, born in Naples but settled in Rome where his poetry acquired much fame. [29]

Suetonius: born c.69 AD, held secretarial posts in the Imperial Palace in Rome; his most famous historical work is *Lives of the Twelve Caesars* (from Julius Caesar to Domitian). [26]

Tacitus: c.55-120 AD, lawyer, politician and historian of the Roman Empire in the 1st century AD. [24,26,30, Ep]

Thucydides: c.460-400 BC, Athenian historian, described the Peloponnesian War (431-404 BC), but his history is incomplete and breaks off in 411 BC. [12,13,14,15, Ep]

Virgil: 70-19 BC, Roman poet; his long epic poem *The Aeneid* has been studied by school pupils from the 1st to the 21st centuries. [25,31]

Xenophon: c.428-354 BC, Greek writer on numerous subjects; his Greek History covers the period 411 (where Thucydides broke off) down to 362 BC. [13,16]

Appendix 2

MAPS OF GREECE AND ITALY

Map of Greece

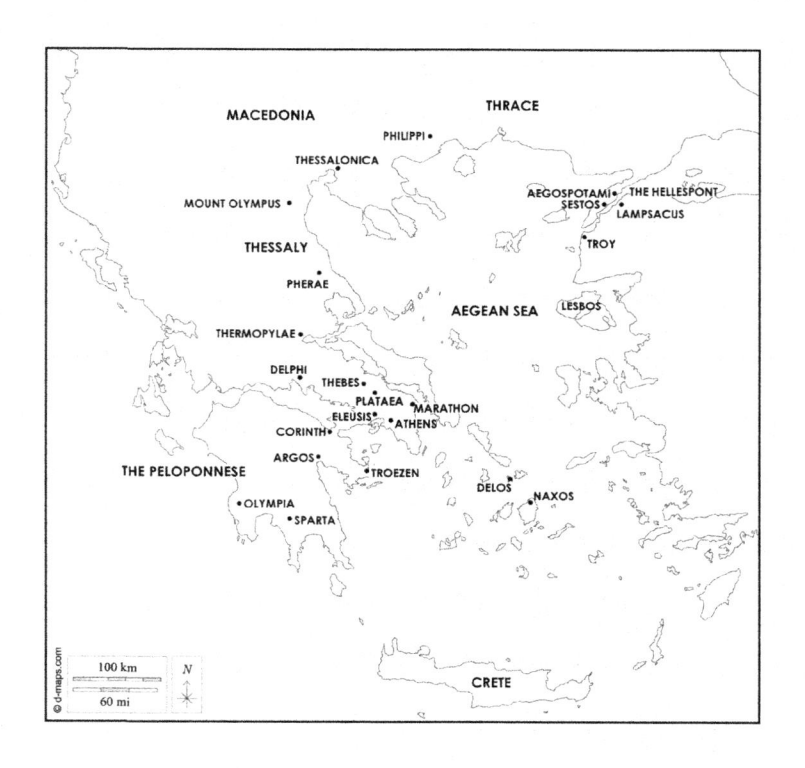

Map of Italy

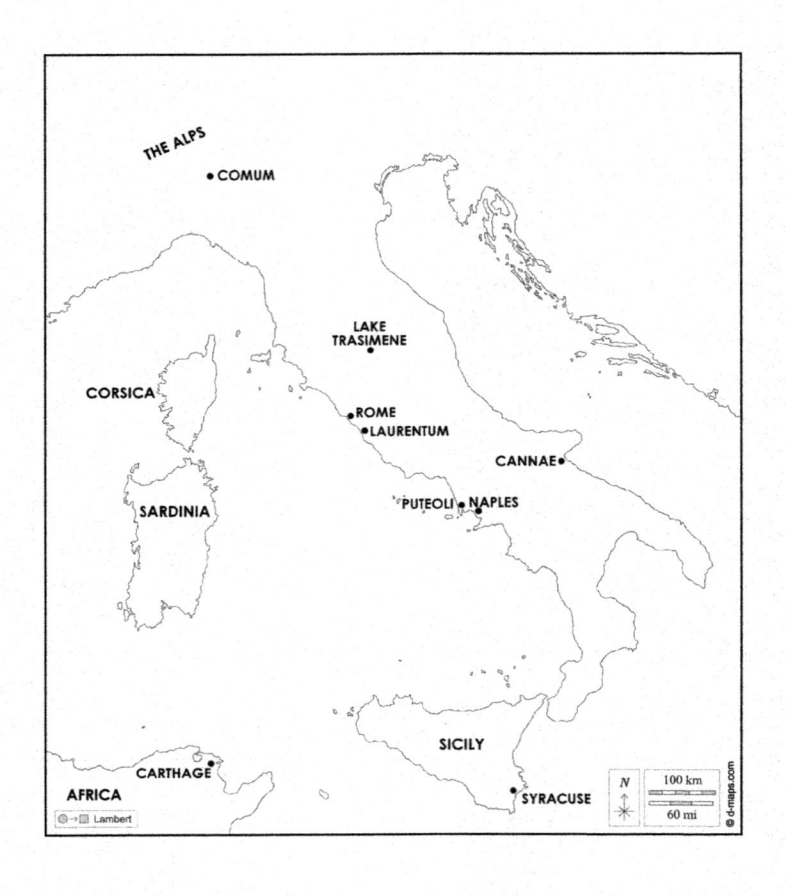

Printed by Printforce, United Kingdom